Nextfest
Anthology II

Plays from the Syncrude Next Generation Arts Festival
2001–2005

Métis Mutt
SHELDON ELTER

Code Word: Time
LEAH SIMONE BOWEN

Beneath the Deep Blue Sky
ROB BARTEL

Grumplestock's
KEVIN JESUINO, TRISH LORENZ, JON STEWART

Citrus
JANIS CRAFT

EDITED BY STEVE PIROT

Prairie Play Series: 25 / Series Editor, Diane Bessai

For individual production rights please contact either the playwrights or Theatre Network at 10708 124th Street, Edmonton, AB, T5M 0H1

Library and Archives Canada Cataloguing in Publication
Nextfest anthology II : plays from the Syncrude Next Generation Arts Festival / edited by Steve Pirot.

(Prairie play series ; 25)

ISBN-13: 978-1-897126-04-2
ISBN-10: 1-897126-04-2

1. Canadian drama (English)—Alberta--Edmonton. 2. Canadian drama (English)—21st century. I. Pirot, Steve, 1968- II. Series.
PS8315.5.P73N492 2006   C812'.608097123   C2006-901148-6

Editor: Steve Pirot
Editor for the Press: Diane Bessai
Cover design: Dale Nigel Goble, based on photo supplied by Nathanael Sapara
Interior photos have been produced with the kind permission of the photographers.

 Canada Council for the Arts   Conseil des Arts du Canada   Canadian Heritage   Patrimoine canadien   edmonton arts council

NeWest Press acknowledges the support of the Canada Council for the Arts and the Alberta Foundation for the Arts, and the Edmonton Arts Council for our publishing program. We also acknowledge the financial support of the Government of Canada through the Book Publishing Industry Development Program (BPIDP) for our publishing activities.

Nextfest Society acknowledges the ongoing support of Syncrude Canada Ltd., Theatre Network, the Department of Canadian Heritage, the Canada Council for the Arts, the Alberta Foundation for the Arts, the Edmonton Arts Council, Enbridge Canada Ltd., DevStudios, Vue Weekly, Big Rock Brewery and the Edmonton Downtown Business Association.

NeWest Press
201–8540–109 Street
Edmonton, Alberta T6G 1E6
(780) 432-9427
www.newestpress.com

1   2   3   4   5   09   08   07   06

PRINTED AND BOUND IN CANADA

A staple element of Nextfest are its play readings through which we offer our audience the opportunity to experience new work in its nascent stages and to participate in the development process. Pictured here is the 2002 reading of *Grimwag* by Ryan Hughes (which was subsequently in NextFest 2003's Mainstage Theatre Program) with Jeff Halaby and Rachel Martens. The paintings on the wall are one half of the visual art exhibit by Sarah Cooke.

Dance curator Kay Grigar performs from her dance /spoken word
piece *Gloss Girl* at Integration Pilates & Open Space Inc.

The first (but not the last) time King Mustafa made
Nextfestians bounce at The Sidetrack Café in 2002.

Contents

Nextfest audience in the Roxy Theatre at the 2005 Opening Ceremonies.
PHOTOGRAPH COURTESY OF NATHANAEL SAPARA

Introduction
The Reign of the Unruly

NEXTFEST 2001–2005: YEARS SIX THROUGH
TEN, THE UNRULY YEARS

Welcome to the second anthology of plays developed and presented through the Syncrude Next Generation Arts Festival—colloquially known as NeXtfest . . . or neXtfest . . . or NeXtFest . . . or Nextfest . . . or nextfest . . . depending on which year you are referring to. Currently we are in favour of the all lowercase letters "nextfest", but nothing is constant except change so don't get used to it. In this volume, however, we pledge a vow to consistency and clarity, and will use the appellation "Nextfest."

This collection represents the five years following NeWest Press' autumn 2000 publication of the first *NeXtFest Anthology*. That book's introduction, written by the first two Nextfest Festival Directors, Glenda Stirling and Bradley Moss, gives a fine sense of the philosophy and history of Nextfest in its first five years, and we heartily refer you to that book with its plays, *Tuesdays and Sundays, The Keys To Violet's Apartment, SuperEd, Benedetta Carlini*, and *"No. Please—"*.

The impulse to foster and promote the work of young artists at the beginning of their careers remained our standard as the festival continued to develop in the years 2001 to 2005 under Festival Director Steve Pirot. Nextfest has grown in many ways since the first anthology, the most significant of which was the expansion of the festival in 2002 from a six-day event to an eleven-day event. This expansion sparked growth in practically all other areas of the festival including audience attendance, artist participation, geographic representation, media coverage, a larger, full-colour program, new Festival Partners, and increased prominence to programming outside our Mainstage Theatre Program. If the sum total of your experience of Nextfest is the book you are holding in your hands, then you might fairly assume that our sole concern is theatre, and indeed Nextfest's dominant reputation is that of a theatre festival featuring new works by young playwrights. However, since its inception in 1996, it has always been multi-disciplinary in its scope of programming. While our Theatre programming grew, so too did our programs of Visual Arts, Dance, Music and Film/Video.

Whittling the selection of plays down to the five here presented from the approximately one hundred new plays that Nextfest gave attention to over the past five years (in our Mainstage Theatre and Play Development Readings Programs) was no small task. The overriding criterion for the selection of the plays in this book was "to compile a representative sample of Nextfest programming over the years of 2001 to 2005." This final selection was never intended as a "best of one hundred" as that would imply competition and Nextfest is not built upon a competitive model: Nextfest is built upon a model of participation.

For instance, all participating artists are given passes for all Nextfest events. As a result the festival has quite naturally become a common ground for artistic exchange. Of course it is impossible to dismiss completely that competitive desire to be "the hit of the festival," but the rhythm of mutual support that permeates the festival is something that Nextfest's audiences and artists understand well; it's very Canadian. Equipped with a mandate of professional development, Nextfest is the hub of a support network that encourages artistic risk and exuberance, and introduces dancers, playwrights, musicians, and actors, to one another, helping to seed new relationships and projects. Nextfest gives young artists of every type and stripe an opportunity to hone their craft in a professionally presented festival. Festival administration takes on the work of production management, marketing, publicity, box office, venue management, etc. so that the emphasis for the artists is to cultivate and attend to their expressive voices.

Nextfest is sexy. As young artists shake off the sleep of academia, Nextfest is opening the theatre doors to them and daring them to take the stage. Edmonton's winter night dream has ended and the long days of June favour chaotic colour. This is the climate in which Nextfest breathes. That the gathering of the Nextfestians occurs at the height of spring is telling. Nextfest is an irrational eleven-day party that celebrates youth, newness, and creativity. It is what the word "festival" implies . . . it is festive. Nextfest is a passionate, silly, irrational, serious, drunken flower articulately flirting with a mirror. It is a rambunctious brat and a prophetic protégé. It's loud and argumentative. It stinks like lilacs. It inspires purple prose. It's addictive. It's fun.

Much of the work that occurs at Nextfest is reminiscent of the early years of the Canadian Fringe Festivals when their artists and audiences exhibited a similar hunger for diversity, invention, and risk. Because (unlike the Fringes) Nextfest is not built upon a free-market model, the fear of financial failure for the individual artist does not exist. That encourages a different idea of risk and responsibility. Nextfest is both a testing ground and a debutante's ball for new work that continues on to subsequent presentation at other festivals and by other producers. We take great pride in the number of productions (not just the scripts but the actual productions) that have prèmiered at Nextfest and then continued on to presentation in Calgary, Vancouver, Whitehorse, Yellowknife, Winnipeg, Toronto, Ottawa, New York, New Mexico, Prague, Edinburgh, Auckland, and elsewhere.

With the addition in 2002 of an extra four days of programming and a second venue (Azimuth Theatre) the capacity of Nextfest's theatre programming has doubled since the first anthology. The geographic range of playwrights represented has expanded to Toronto, Newfoundland, New York, Chicago,

North Carolina, and Australia. We initiated the production of plays written by high-school playwrights. We experimented with putting theatre into the hands of dance artists and vice versa. We put musicians, painters, and the audience on stage with actors. We've staged plays in nightclubs.

However, this introduction would be an incomplete representation of the big picture without noting the growth in the other arts served by the festival (dance, music, visual art, film, inter-disciplinary, etc). The following curators employed their own brand of passion and commitment to enlarging and improving their programs: Saskia Aarts (Visual Arts); Clinton Carew, Lindsay McIntyre, David Cheoros, David Gates (Film); Amy Schindel, Kay Grigar, Linda Turnbull (Dance); Bradley Moss, Chris Martin (Music). There were the special theatre program coordinators Matt Kowalchuk, Morgan Smith (Play Shorts); Sarah Hoyles (Solo-liloquies). There were inter-disciplinary projects led by Paul Blain (*wonderland*), Michael Chyz (*Neverwhere*), Juliann Wilding (*p[ART]y*), Sarah Bowes (*Just Press Play*), Aaron Talbot *(Ina Garden uv Hedons Baby)*. Other projects were guided by Lynette Bodnarchuk of the Edmonton Small Press Association (*The X-Press Book Project*), Philip Jagger (*emergence*), Carol Murray-Gilchrist (Multi-Youth Productions), and Keri Ekberg (iHuman Youth Society), and Nextfest superstar Ottillie Parfitt (High School Mentorship Coordinator). Finally there were the diverse new initiatives headed up by Nextfest founder, Bradley Moss (Live Radio Broadcasts and The Amazing Play Creation Day).

The Visual Arts component of Nextfest grew enormously especially under the supervision of Saskia Aarts who assumed the curatorship in 2002. The number of venues increased, outreach to local artists deepened, while artists representing Toronto, Vancouver, and Calgary increased the geographic scope of the program. The presentation values matured significantly and as a result the quality of submissions reached a higher level.

We have also enjoyed presenting partnerships with Latitude 53, iHuman Arts Society, The Society of Student Artists, and the Nina Haggerty Centre For The Arts.

For the first seven years the music component of Nextfest was curated by Bradley Moss, followed in 2002 by Chris Martin. The music component is composed of a series in the lobby of the Roxy Theatre for songwriters, and the Bands Around Town series through which we are invited into the local watering holes that still present live musicians (most notably The Sidetrack Café). We have seen the likes of Chris Demeanor, Maren Ord, Wendy McNeil, Rachelle Van Zanten, King Muskafa (our resident closing party band), Ann Vriend, AA Sound System, Daisy Blue Groff, Proxyboy, Ben Spencer, Red Shag Carpet, Eshod Ibyn Wyza, Kim Barlow and Andrea House.

The dance component of Nextfest has seen three curators between 2001 and 2005 (Amy Schindel, Kay Grigar, and Linda Turnbull) each who have found ways to increase the presence of the art form within the larger structure of the festival. Amy was the initial instigator who insisted that Nextfest should have a consistent and stable dance component. Kay cast the Nextfest net further and deeper by concentrating on the mentorship needs of local dancers while inviting dance from Montreal. Linda broadened Nextfest's dance program even further with an increase to the number of dance presentations in the program and solid representation from the west coast.

What began in 1996 as a six-day event showcasing the work of approximately one hundred artists with a decided focus on new plays by young playwrights is now an eleven-day event showcasing the work of approximately four hundred and fifty artists with an increased attention to artists in most every art form. Audience attendance has grown seven-fold and similarly our presence in the media, on the web (a huge thank you to DevStudios for that), and each year more and more young artists from around the world become aware of our unique event.

Every year we see something new: a way of collaborating, an incorporation of technology, poetry jams, six-hour long collective creations, fashion as art, a do-it-yourself 'zine, painting as performance, plays with cast sizes upward of fifty, bagpipes, capoeira, nudity, zombie attacks, and parties that won't end until the sun comes up. However, the primary attention and reputation of Nextfest is still that of a new works theatre festival and thus a volume of scripts is still the most appropriate means of representing the festival in book form.

As stated above, this is not a "best of Nextfest 2001–2005" as much as it is a "some of Nextfest 2001–2005." With its variety of contemporary styles and themes, this collection of five plays stand for the serious passion and itching need of legions of Nexfestians. This book is only a glimpse of the diversity of voices, and the boldness of expression that we have been privileged to oversee at our festival for the past ten years.

Soak in it

Rock on.

Steve Pirot   Bradley Moss
Festival Director   Festival Producer
Edmonton, January 2006

A very consistent presence at Nextfest in its first ten years has been the
collectively created musicals of Multi-Youth Productions under the
guidance of Carol Murray-Gilchrist and James Chilchrist.
Pictured here at the Roxy Theatre is *Plastic Flowers*, their 2002
play based on manufactured pop music.

Nextfest has programs that attend to the typical disciplines but we
also like to experiment with form, venue, and audience such as in
the multi-disciplinary night club theatre event *Neverwhere*.
Produced by Michael Chyz, the evening included installations,
dancers, actors, bands, Society for Creative Anachronism combat,
audience interaction, shadow play, wall noise, and more all in the
environment of New City Suburbs old location on 112th Street.

Sheldon Elter in his autobiographical play *Métis Mutt.*
PHOTOGRAPH COURTESY OF DAVID WILLIAMSON

Métis Mutt

Sheldon Elter

INTRODUCTION

Métis Mutt began as part of a class exercise in Grant MacEwan Community College's Theatre Arts Program. As a culminating exercise for his first-year students, Ken Brown conducts an exercise called 'Vocal Mask' in which the actors choose a theme and work independently towards the creation of a ten-minute piece. Ken encourages the students to improvise without pen and paper and to avoid telling a story. In 2001 I was unable to attend their final class presentation so I asked Ken what I would be missing. That was the first time I heard the name Sheldon Elter. Ken is an artist and teacher for whom I have great admiration and his passionate advocacy for Sheldon's piece was all I needed to hear. I contacted the curator of Nextfest's Shorts Program (Matthew Kowalchuk) and told him that we had a Ken Brown recommendation. This is how the first version of *Métis Mutt* came to be a part of NeXtFest 2001.

That ten-minute piece made a splash in the Edmonton theatre scene that year, and as Sheldon, Ken, I myself, and Edmonton wanted to see more of this story, we started talking about a fully developed stand-alone version of *Métis Mutt* to prèmiere at NeXtFest 2002. Ken and Sheldon got to work and so it came to be. The show was presented at two venues (the Roxy and Azimuth) and had no scenic elements whatsoever with the exception of a guitar stand and a microphone stand. There were no costume changes and minimal use of props, lights, and sound to support the character transformations of the actor.

The stories in *Métis Mutt* are clearly autobiographical, but there is more to the show than that. Autobiographical shows are often tagged "based on real life experiences" as if that automatically guarantees truth and authenticity. It does not. The authenticity of *Métis Mutt* is largely due to its artifice and artistic vision; artistic integrity takes precedence over real life verity. However, the fact that it is autobiographical is not irrelevant, especially when you get to experience Sheldon performing. There is something sacred about the depiction of Sheldon-the-character that

Sheldon-the-performer leads us through that is different than reading the script (or having it performed by somebody else). That authenticity extends to the characters other than "Sheldon" as well because no matter how effective and complete his character transformations are, it is always understood that there really is only one character in the show and that is Sheldon Elter.

After its prèmiere at Nextfest, *Métis Mutt* had a run at the 2002 Edmonton Fringe and Azimuth Theatre toured the play to secondary schools (with a sanitized version of the script which was accomplished in consultation with then Artistic Director Christopher Craddock). The Fringe production received Elizabeth Sterling Haynes Awards for Outstanding Fringe New Work and Outstanding Fringe Performance By An Actor. It was at the Fringe that Mary Vingoe saw the show and invited it to the inaugural version of the Magnetic North Theatre Festival in Ottawa. *Métis Mutt* has since been performed in the Yukon, North West Territories, Nova Scotia, New Zealand and back home in Edmonton at the Roxy Theatre.

It cannot be overstated that much of the success of *Métis Mutt* is due to Sheldon's skills as an actor, comic, singer, mimic, and storyteller. Without those skills and a requisite emotional distance from the experiences being conveyed, *Métis Mutt* would probably read merely as art therapy. It is not. The personal nature of the story creates a special kind of intimacy but the experience of the show is not ceremonial nor is it ritual. It is an artistic storytelling experience. This is also true of other one-person autobiographical shows at Nextfest that (not coincidentally) Sheldon has a hand in developing. He directed and dramaturged Jeremy Baumung's *Dead Man Talking* for a reading at NextFest 2003 and directed its production at Azimuth Theatre the following autumn. *Dead Man Talking* was nominated for a Sterling Award for Outstanding New Work, and has had similar touring success at the Ignite Festival in Auckland, and Stuck In A Snowbank in Yellowknife. Sheldon also developed and directed Kristi Hansen's *Woody* which was in the Mainstage Theatre program at nextfest 2005.

– S.P.

At NeXtFest 2001 *Métis Mutt* was first presented as a ten-minute piece as part of the Xtra Large Shorts Program (curated by Matthew Kowalchuk) in the Roxy Theatre.

At NeXtFest 2002 the first full-length version of *Métis Mutt* was presented at both the Roxy Theatre and Azimuth Theatre and subsequently at the Edmonton International Fringe Theatre Festival 2002. The production team was as follows:

Playwright/Performer: *Sheldon Elter*
Production Advisor/Dramaturge: *Ken Brown*
Stage Manager: *Jeremy Baumung*

With assistance from Chris Craddock, a high school adaptation was toured by Azimuth Theatre to schools across the province of Alberta in the autumn of 2002 with Bobby Smale serving as road manager.

Kristi Hansen served as stage manager when *Métis Mutt* went to the 2003 Magnetic North Theatre Festival in Ottawa and the On The Waterfront Festival in Dartmouth, Nova Scotia. Jeremy returned as Stage Manager for runs at the Nakai Comedy Festival in Whitehorse, and the AK03 Festival in Auckland, New Zealand.

In November 2003, *Métis Mutt* returned to the Roxy Theatre to be presented by Theatre Network as part of the 2003/2004 season. For this production, new design elements were incorporated including lights by Bobby Smale and a backdrop created by Angie Sotiropoulos. The Stage Manager was Rachel Livingstone.

In autumn 2004, Jeremy and Sheldon served as one another's stage managers when both *Métis Mutt* and *Dead Man Talking* were presented by Stuck In A Snowbank Theatre in Yellowknife, North West Territories.

THE CHARACTERS

There is one character, **Sheldon Elter**, adopting many personas.

THE SETTING

There is virtually no setting. The locations of the story are indicated by the actor.

Jeff Halaby, Bequie Lake, Kristi Hansen, Sheldon Elter, and Ken Brown
hanging out post-show in the lobby of the Roxy Theatre.
PHOTOGRAPH COURTESY OF DAVID WILLIAMSON

Métis Mutt

Note: *The play opens with Sheldon the Comedian performing some of his early stand-up material, which is very racist.
At first, the audience may find him funny, but as the routine
progresses, the coarseness of the material begins to escalate and
the negative stereotypes he displays of aboriginal culture trans-
form the audience's laughter into disgust, and shock. As the play
unfolds, Sheldon's adverse circumstances growing up between
two cultures are revealed. The audience witnesses the growth of
the young, ignorant comedian, as well as his spiritual growth
and self-actualisation into manhood, that provides him with
the knowledge, and freedom to make positive change in his life.
Sheldon recalls and relives his journey much the same way the
human memory works, by leaping back and forth through time,
and combining multiple character sketches with storytelling.
The piece is based on true tales from his life, although some stories have been slightly altered for theatrical purposes.*

*Stage left: A microphone and stand, an electric acoustic guitar
on a stand. This is Sheldon the Comedian's performing area, in
spotlight during stand-up and singing.*

*Centre stage: There is a chair and an eagle feather lying under-
neath. Almost all of the action takes place here.*

*Stage right: This is where Sheldon speaks to his father, Sonny,
represented by a warm, amber light.*

*Top of show, house lights are out, a jazzy, but cheesy comedy
club intro recording begins. . . .*

Club Announcer Voice: Ladies and gentlemen, welcome to
amateur night at The Comedy Club. Please welcome, for
his first appearance on our stage . . . Sheldon Elter.

BAD COMEDY

Sheldon: Hello, My name is Sheldon Elter, and I'll be your
Native comedian for this evening. But that's just my stage
name. I'm actually Sheldon Elter Wanotch L'hirondelle
Johnson Black Laboucan Cardinal Smith. I kept all those
names out of respect for my dads.

My mom told me to use that one.

So please understand that I am Métis. Which means that I'm Native, AND White. So half of me wants to, *bad British accent,* "assimilate you into my culture", and the other half is, *thick Native accent,* "just too lazy to do it." Now, I know I don't look that Native . . . my skin's not that dark, I don't have the long braids . . . and I'm working . . . but I am PART Native, and PART White. Just don't ask me which parts . . . I'm a little ashamed. . . . Wouldn't it be great if you could just pick your parts, "I'll have the black one." I love my people. We are a very close people. That's why you can fit fifty of us in a car.

I grew up in a small town, which is hard, because you're related to everybody. Once, I actually dated my cousin. What can you say in a situation like that? *Does a doggy style spanking motion.* "Who's your cousin, who's your cousin?" Growing up in a small town, there's always those guys with the big trucks and the big stereos . . . *Makes "umph-ing" sounds of loud bass woofers.* I had that. I had a brand new Ford F-150 by the time I was sixteen, and I didn't even have to pay for it. So while I have the chance, I'd like to thank all you taxpayers out there . . . Thank you.

My grandfather was a very wise man. His name was Harry Hurting Hoop. He used to tell me this old Indian proverb, "Ni husco awa paysoom," which means, "Never ride a bicycle without a seat."

My mom isn't as Native as my father, but she still tries to teach me things about Indians. One time I brought a girl over, and my mom asked, "Do you know how an Indian stretches a beaver? Like this." *Obscene gesture.*

My girlfriend just went on birth control . . . but not to stop her from getting pregnant, it was just so she could receive the "Crime Stoppers" award. I dated a black girl once, but we decided it probably wasn't a good idea to mate because then our kids would be too lazy to steal.

ONE-LINERS

These jokes begin lightly, and gradually increase in tempo.

What do you call an Indian on a bike? Thief!

What do you call two Indians on a bike? Organized Crime.

Why don't you ever hit an Indian on a bike? 'Cause it might be your bike.

What did the little Indian boy across the street get for his birthday? Your bike.

What do you call forty squaws in a room? A full set of teeth.

What's the definition of confusion? Father's day on the reserve.

Where's the best place to hide an Indian's welfare cheque? Under his workboots.

Delivering faster.

Why did God give seagulls wings? So they could beat the Indians to the dump.

Why did the Indian cross the road? To sleep in the other ditch.

How do you get an Indian to take a bath? Throw his welfare cheque in the water.

How do you get him out? Throw in a bar of soap.

Why are there only two pallbearers at an Indian's funeral? Garbage cans only have two handles.

How do you wink at an Indian? *Gesture of aiming rifle.*

Beat.

What did Jesus say to the Indians before he died? Don't do anything 'til I get back.

Lights fade. Sheldon moves centre stage in front of chair. Lights up.

INSULTS

Attention-Getter: Hey! Ya Indian!

Tough Guy: Fuckin' Indian!

War Cry Girl: *Hand tapping motion making war cry sound, then:* Redskin!

Taunter: Tonto!

Joker: Squaw!

Hick: Wagon-burner!

Dancer: *Chug-a-lug drinking motion while doing mock tribal dance.* Chug-a-lug! Chug-a-lug! Chug-a-lug!

Fade lights, moves stage right. Amber light.

DEAR DADDY

Little Sheldon: *About five years old.*

> Dear Daddy,
> I had fun at my visit to your house. I like Edmonton. Uncle Doug took me to Fantasyland, and I rode in a boat, a BIG boat that swings, and went and played in all these balls.
> I liked watching TV and having Spam and mustard sandwiches with you. I was really scared when you fell over and were shaking and choking. I don't know any phone numbers in Edmonton. I was mad at mom for taking me away again. I want to be with YOU.
> Dad, can you and mom please stop fighting and make things better? Then we can live in the same house again. I miss you and I hope you feel better.
> Love,
> Sheldon

Fade lights, as Sheldon moves to centre, lights shift.

SOMETHING HAPPENED TO ME IN 1999

Sheldon: Something strange happened to me in 1999. Actually, a lot of very strange things happened to me in 1999, beginning with the death of my father, Sonny L'hirondelle, on New Year's Eve, and then a weird spiral downward, and the opening of a door whose existence I hadn't previously suspected. But . . . I'll get to that later. . . .

Snap light change.

Racist Coward: Hey, Elter! Hey, Geronimo! Yeah, YOU! Ya heathen! Savage! Prairie nigger! Bush nigger! NAVAHO!

Suddenly scared, and begins making excuses. No, I'm not saying all Indians are bad people . . . just the ones who give them a bad name. *Really scared now that he is about to get beat up.* No, I'm not saying YOU'RE one of those people. I don't want to fight you.

Step-Dad: *Loud, booming Native voice, pointing down at Little Sheldon.* Stop your cryin'! You want something to cry about? I'm sick and tired of this shit. The next time, *Grabs Young Sheldon's arm, and demonstrates, twisting his arm behind him, forcing Young Sheldon to the floor,* you take his arm, and you put it behind his head, and you hold it there 'til it snaps. Make him cry, 'cause the next time you come home cryin', you're gettin' a goddamn, good lickin'!

Little Sheldon: Bro', we don't have to fight all the time.

Little Brother Derek: *Crying, rubbing his eyes.* But he called me an Indian!

Little Sheldon: But Derek, we ARE Indians . . . STOP CRYING!

MY DAD KIDNAPPED ME

Long, slow fade to small area in front of chair. Cool, blue light as if evening is approaching.

Sheldon: My dad kidnapped me once. I was just old enough to remember. It's one of my first memories. He took me to someone's trailer, where a party was going on. Everyone was drinking. My dad was playing the guitar with his usual incredible skill. He had a knack for still being able to play lead guitar while not actually being able to walk from the alcohol. *Sits on the floor.* I was put in a bedroom, and told to sleep. I awoke to a rustling noise. My father and some woman were beside me. When they realized I was awake, they stopped what they were doing. They were naked. I saw her breasts and didn't recognize what they were. So I asked.

Drunken Woman: *On her knees, holding her breasts, showing him.* They're pillows. You can play with them.

Young Sheldon: She put my hands on them. *Young Sheldon, confused, slowly reaches forward to touch her breasts.*

Light change.

Elder: *Rises slowly to his feet, addressing a group.* Women are sacred. When we're walkin' around inside the teepee, we walk behind the women outta respect. We give great respect to Mother Earth, and to women in general, as they are the givers of life.

Snap to red top lighting.

Sonny: *Slaps Mom, while holding her by the collar.* You bitch! *Slaps her again, choking her down to the floor, pointing, and threatening Young Sheldon.* Sheldon! You touch that phone, and I'll kill you! Go ahead. Call the police.

Light change.

Mom: *On the phone, wiping blood from her nose.* Hi, Dolly. No, he kicked me out again. He left me with nothing. I've got no milk or diapers for Derek. Thank you.

Young Sheldon: *Rising to his feet, looking up at his Mom.* Mom, when me and Derek grow up, we're gonna get big like Arnold Schwarznegger, and beat Dad up for you.

Light change.

POST-PARTY EXTRACTS

Sheldon: I remember cleaning up after a party my Dad and his friends had at our house in Grande Prairie. *Pulls back chair.* Mom and I moved the couch back to see what was behind it. *Picks up an imaginary bottle.* Every single one of her extracts for cooking had been drunk.

Fade lights.

Sound of a club, audience noise. Comedian spotlight up as Sheldon moves to mic, stage left. He picks up the guitar, nervously, and plays, twelve bar blues.

SONG: I LIKE THE BOOZE

> I passed out in summer
> Woke up in the fall
> It must have been that case of Lysol

I like the booze
I like the booze
Well you don't know what drunk is
'Til you've walked a mile in my shoes

One night I drank some Malibu
Some Aqua Velva too
The next morning I woke up
In bed with a caribou

I like the booze
I like the booze
Well you don't know what drunk is
'Til you've walked a mile in my shoes

One morning I woke up in a cardboard box
Cops put me in detox
They kicked me out for drinkin'
Fluid from the Xerox

I like the booze
I like the booze
Well you don't know what drunk is
'Til you've walked a mile in my shoes

Sheldon ends with a riff that we are to hear again. Sound of applause. Spotlight fades. Moves to centre, becoming a shy, meek, Native woman. Slowly picks up the eagle feather, and begins to speak as if at a sharing circle.

Native Woman: *Thick rez accent.* Thank you for letting me speak. I just want to say that I really enjoyed Sheldon's comedy . . . *Begins to cry* . . . but I just don't think he should say bad things about our people. My father did terrible things to me and my sister. *Slowly puts the feather back down. Turns upstage, when he sits in chair, lights change immediately.*

THE FIGHT WITH GLASSES

Sheldon: I'm eight years old, grade two. My little brother Derek is five. It's lunchtime. Sonny made soup with leftovers in it.

Young Sheldon: Dad, I don't want this stuff in my soup. It's gross.

Sonny: Okay, my boy. I'll strain it for you.

Derek: I don't want this stuff either.

Sonny: YOU'LL goddamn well eat it!

Sheldon: I rarely got a lickin' from Sonny, but he beat Derek all the time.

Mom: *Sitting, applying makeup.* Now, Sonny, that's not fair.

Sonny stands up, and reaches across the table and slaps her. Falls in chair as Mom, and receives the slap.

Sheldon: *Acting this out in slow motion.* She was getting ready for work. She picked up her mirror and threw it at him. It grazed his shoulder and shattered against the wall. Derek, barefooted and barely dressed, ran outside.

Young Sheldon: *Gets up, and runs around the chair, chasing after Derek, catches him, and bends down to speak to him.* Derek, I want you to ride your bike to Auntie Evelyn's all right? *Moves behind chair, and climbs onto it, crouching.* I went to my favourite hiding place on top of the garage. I can see in the window. They're still fighting. I'm a coward. What can I do? What can I do? I have to see if she's okay. *Climbs off the chair, slowly creeping around and in front of the chair.* They are in the living room. I peek around the corner so he doesn't see me. *He mimes this.* Mom is crying and holding her glasses in her hand. She stands still, keeping her head down, and he's yelling things at her. *Mimes Sonny slapping Mom.* Then without looking up . . . *Miming Mother's actions in slow motion . . .* she throws her glasses at him. As he flinches, she smokes him in the face! He falls to the couch. *He does this, then shows us Mom's actions. . . .* She jumped on top of him, putting her elbow on his throat, choking him. *He makes choking sound.* She begins to punch him. I run back outside. She comes out, and we climb in the truck to leave.

Mom: *Sits in chair, starts the truck, then stops.* Shel, mommy can't drive without her glasses. Can you go in and get them . . . Sheldon, please!

Young Sheldon: *Creeping into the living room.* Dad, can I have mom's glasses, please?

Sheldon: He had a bloody, fat lip, bumps on his forehead, a bloody nose, and his glasses were twisted on his face. He just sat there, motionless, and quiet. *Becomes Sonny, sitting in post-fight emptiness.*

Young Sheldon: *Stands, and slowly bends picking up the glasses.* I picked them up off the floor.

A last image of him standing, looking at Sonny. He sits in the chair, lights, and character shifts instantly.

SHELDON AND LEANNE'S GRANDMOTHER ON THE PHONE

Sound: Phone rings.

Grandmother: *Very old, heavy Native accent.* Hello?

Sheldon: Hello, is Leanne there?

Grandmother: She's just girl.

Sheldon: No, no, Mrs. Hamlin, it's me, Sheldon. I'm Pat's son. I helped you carry your groceries in yesterday.

Grandmother: She's just girl. You leave her alone. *Hangs up.*

Sound: Phone rings.

Grandmother: Hello?

Sheldon: Is Leanne there?

Grandmother: No. She wassin' her hair. *Hangs up.*

Sound: Phone rings.

Grandmother: Hello?

Sheldon: Is Leanne there?

Grandmother: *Long pause.* Ya. *Slowly, and deliberately hangs up.*

Lights.

IN THE SWEATLODGE

Sheldon: When I was about eighteen, I was working for the Sagitawa Friendship Centre in Peace River. I was a camp councillor for these Native kids, twelve to seventeen years old. One of the activities for the kids was a traditional sweat ceremony. We were supposed to fast for four days, but only fasted for one. On the reserve, we met Bill Newski, the Medicine Man. He told us we weren't allowed to wear any metal, for religious reasons, and because it could burn you. *Lights dim, as he picks up the drum, and the eagle feather. Ceremoniously, he sits on the floor cross-legged, miming this.* The fireman dropped some rocks into the pit, and closed the door. Bill put some cedar, sage, and sweet grass onto the rocks. You could see it burn. *Using feather.* Then he fanned it with what looked like a hawk or an eagle wing, passed around a pipe, which we smoked out of. Then he held his drum over the rocks to tighten the skin.

Bill: *Ladling water onto the rocks, making hissing sound on each of the following.* Hiss!; One to the east; hiss!; one to the west; hiss!; one to the north; hiss!; one to the south.

Sheldon: And the lodge got hotter and hotter. He said some prayers, and sang a few songs. Every now and then, the fireman would drop more hot rocks onto the pit. Then he passed around drums, rattles, sticks.

Bill: I'm gonna sing a song in Cree, and even if you don't know what I'm singin', if you feel the urge to sing, go right ahead.

Sheldon takes the drum, awkwardly, and begins to sing, then starts to cry.

Person Beside Sheldon: Are you okay, man?

Sheldon: Then one of the girls wanted to get out. . . .

Girl: *Panicked.* I can't take it! I can't take it!

Bill: It's okay. You'll be all right. We can't open the door because the spirits will be scared away by the light, and it will ruin the ceremony. It's cooler on the bottom. Put your face to Mother Earth.

Sheldon: She did, and she was okay. At the end, he was saying a final prayer, and he sprinkled some more sage on the rocks. *Using feather.* He began to fan the rocks with the wing, and I could feel this fanning come from close to my face, you could hear feathers flapping, "fump-fump, fump-fump", next to my face. I'm flinching and backing away from the heat, and I can feel the feathers hitting my face, which was impossible, because he was on the opposite side of the lodge, a good six feet away with a pit full of hot rocks between us. There was no way he could have reached across. When we got out, I asked him . . . "What were you doing, fanning and touching me with that big wing you had?"

Bill: What are you talking about?"

Sheldon: And the girl, who had been beside me, said . . .

Girl: Ya, I felt it too.

Bill: Well, no, I wasn't touching you. *Smiles knowingly.* This was a blessing. You've been blessed.

Sheldon: *Surreptitiously to Bill.* Hey Bill, when we were singing that song, I started crying at the end . . . it wasn't like I was sad or anything. It was just coming out.

Bill: Hmmm. You should go out into the wilderness, where you can't have any physical contact with anybody. Take the basic necessities, and stay there for however long you feel you need to. Your spirit is grieving. You should stay out there until you've dealt with whatever it is you're hanging onto. A spirit quest.

Sheldon: And I thought, "ridiculous." First of all, where does a guy find the time to just take off for weeks, or months? I didn't see how you would be dealing with things by just staying out in the wilderness.

I had been doing stand-up comedy in Grande Prairie, while going to college, and had played at Yuk Yuk's in Edmonton. My friend Marc Savard, was performing as a hypnotist. He hired me for his tour, and let me open for him.

Marc Savard: Sheldon, I think you should totally milk your Native heritage here. It's what separates you from all other comedians. People will already appreciate your talents because you play guitar. Hey, you should write a parody of a Christmas song.

Sheldon the Comedian: I don't know, man. We've only got like, ten minutes before I have to go on. I probably wouldn't be able to remember it all anyway.

Marc Savard: If you tell yourself that you will forget, you will. Come on! It would be funny!

Sheldon the Comedian: Well, . . . I could do the Twelve Days of Christmas.

Marc Savard: An INDIAN Twelve Days of Christmas!

Sheldon the Comedian: . . . Okay.

Sound: of club, audience noise. Comedian spotlight up as Sheldon moves to mic, stage left. He picks up the guitar, and plays . . .

TWELVE DAYS OF CHRISTMAS PARODY

On the first day of Christmas, the government gave to me
A squaw passed out under a tree
On the second day of Christmas, the government gave to me
Two bingo dabbers, and a squaw passed out under a tree

. . . and so on, a la "Twelve Days of Christmas" . . .

Three different dads . . .
Four stolen bikes . . .
Five welfare cheques . . .
On the sixth day of Christmas, the government gave to me
A tribal Christmas party

Stops, and is now very drunk through the rest of the song.

On the twelfth day of Christmas, the government gave to me . . .
A wake-up call from the party
There were five welfare cheques, four stolen bikes, three different dads, two bingo dabbers, and a squaw passed out under a tree.

Sound: of applause. Spotlight fades. Moves to centre, lights up.

FIGHT WITH EX-CON

Sheldon: I'm fourteen years old. I was at a girl's birthday party. My cousin Wes, my step-brother Henry Jr., our friend Travis and I were walking some girls home. We decided to take a shortcut through an empty lot. Wes was tossing rocks at signs as we walked.

Teen Sheldon: I bet you can't hit that one.

Picks up a rock, takes aim, and throws. Sound: rock hitting fence, causing a big dog to start barking.

Drunk Ex-Con: Who threw a rock at my dog?!?!??

Sheldon: My cousin and my brother bolt. The guy moves to Travis.

Ex-Con: Was it you??? *Punching him.* Huh?? Huh??

Sheldon: *Miming this.* And he knees him in the head, kicking, and punching him. Travis, on the ground, yells—

Travis: No!! No!! It wasn't me!!

Sheldon: Travis gets up and bolts. I'm still standing there, in front of the girls—

Ex-Con: *Pointing.* Was it you, Sheldon?

Sheldon: Then I realized who it was. It was this eighteen year-old Native guy who lived down our street. He had already been in jail.

Ex-Con: *Holding Sheldon by the collar, threatening to hit him.* Was it you??? Huh?? Huh??

Teen Sheldon: *Being socked in the chin.* No, no, it wasn't me.

Ex-Con: Who was it then??

Sheldon: Right as he was about to hit me, one of the girls stepped between us and he hit her. *Mimes all this.* He started punching my stomach. I grabbed his hair, putting him in a front headlock, choking him, and started punching. He tried to lift me, but couldn't, and we fell to the ground. He was on top of me, so I quickly grabbed two handfuls of his long hair and pulled him in close so he couldn't hit me. Then I see two women coming, his mom and his sister. His mom grabbed MY hair, banging my head on the ground ... *Grabs his own hair, and bangs the back of his head on the floor a few times.*

Ex-Con's Mom: Let go of his hair!! Let go of his hair!!

Sheldon: *Still miming.* I threw him, kicked him, and started to run. My auntie lived close by, so I stopped there.

Teen Sheldon: *Sound: of doorbell ringing several times.* Auntie! Let me in! There's this guy trying to beat me up!

Sheldon: She let me in and closed the door. *Sound: doorbell rings.* It was him.

Ex-Con: Tell Sheldon to come out so I can kick his ass! He threw a rock at my dog!!

Sheldon: My little round auntie stood between us in the doorway.

As Auntie, mean look on her face, slowly, and cautiously opens the door a bit, trying to hide Teen Sheldon behind her.

Teen Sheldon: *Shouting over Auntie's shoulder.* Look, it was my cousin Weslee, if it matters!

Ex-Con: You're fuckin' dead, Sheldon!

Sheldon: My auntie called my mom and said she was taking me to the cop shop. She got my five year-old cousin out of bed and, we drove to the police station, but no one was there. She turned around. Then, coming the other way was a huge car, chasing Wes, swerving occasionally to hit him. My Auntie whipped a nut, passed them, and stopped the car as I opened the door for Wes to jump in. Then the guy slides across the back of the trunk like something out of a movie. He runs beside the car, no shirt, cowboy boots, and wranglers, kicking the door and punching the window. They chased us down Main street, and all the way back to my house. As my Auntie pulled into our crescent, she laid on the horn. *Does this as Auntie, peers over steering wheel. Sound of a long car horn. Then as Sheldon:* My mom and step-dad were immediately outside. My step-dad with only jeans on, and my mom with a see-through nightgown with nothing on underneath.

Ex-Con: Let Sheldon outside!!

Teen Sheldon: *Trying to get past step-dad, Henry, who is holding him back.* Dad, let me outside! I can take this guy!

Ex-Con: You're fuckin' dead, Sheldon!!

Teen Sheldon: *Steps beside step-dad in the doorway, yelling, doing obscene gesture.* Fuck you, fag!

Henry: *Pushes Teen Sheldon back in.* You stay inside!

Sheldon: His mom, screamed at my mom:

Ex-Con's Mom: We're gonna put your son in a pine box!! YOU WHITE WHORE!!

Last image of Ex-Con's mom pointing. Light change.

NEW YEAR'S DAY

Sheldon: I told you that 1999 was a very important year for me. On New Year's Day, my girlfriend, Twila, and I were up in Grimshaw, having dinner with my folks.

Sound: phone rings.

Mom: Hello? Oh, hi Karen . . . What? . . . That's great! . . . I'll tell the boys! . . . Thanks, Karen. *Hangs up.* Derek! Sheldon! Your Dad, Sonny, is going to be over at Robert and Karen's tonight. Uncle Vern, and a bunch of guys who used to play with him are already there. Uncle Chub's son, Randy, is bringing your Dad down from Grande Prairie. Shel, why don't you and Twila come over to Robert and Karen's? You can introduce her to your father, and you and Derek can play guitar with them.

Sheldon: Mom, we were planning to drive to Hines Creek to visit Twila's folks.

Mom: Just call Twila's parents and let them know that you'll be a little late.

Sheldon moves to stage left and brings the guitar centre stage, and sits in the chair.

Sheldon: So we headed over to Robert and Karen's, and played guitar with the guys while we waited for my Dad to show up. *Plays and sings* "Just good old boys . . . " . . . After an hour . . . *Plays* "I ain't makin' no headlines here without you . . . " . . . After two hours . . . *Plays the riff we heard at the end of "I Like the Booze"* . . . Hour three . . .

Young Man Sheldon: Fuck it, mom. I should have known better. *Puts the guitar back on the stand, stage left, and returns to the chair.* Fuck. I'm sorry, Twila. Now your parents have been waiting for nothing. Goodbye everybody. Happy New Year's.

Sheldon: *Lights change, as he sits in chair, driving:* We're fifteen minutes out of Grimshaw, when suddenly . . . a coyote jumps out of the ditch! *Sheldon swerves to miss it, and slams on the brakes. Sound of screeching tires, and a thud. Pulls over, parks, gets out of the car, and slowly walks around the chair, inspecting the car . . .* No damage. *Gets back in the car, puzzled.* We were at Twila's folks' place not even five minutes. . . .

Sound: phone rings.

Twila's Mom: *On the phone.* Hello? . . . Yes . . . Oh . . . God . . . Twila . . . come here.

Twila and her mom have a short, intense discussion about who is to break the news to Sheldon.

Twila's Mom: Sheldon, your father was in an accident just off the Dunvegan Bridge. He's dead.

Light change.

SHELDON BECOMES A HIGH-SCHOOL DRUNK

Sheldon: I never wanted to be like my father. I even changed my last name to Elter, which was okay with my mom, because it said "Elter" on my birth certificate. I never liked the guitar, because he played it, but I learned. In high school . . .

Light change.

High-School Girl: Sheldon, are you going to the party at Claude's house?

Sheldon very drunk, staggers, and sits in chair, then passes out.

Claude: *French accent, high-school student, angry.* Who is this guy on my couch?

David: Ah . . . that's my best friend, Sheldon, man.

Claude: Well he's a fucking cochon. We already had to drag him out of the bathroom because he was passed out in there. Get me the clippers! We're shaving his head!

David: Seetoo, man! Some guys are going to shave Sheldon's head! He's passed out on the couch, man!

Seetoo: *Blocking Claude from getting to Sheldon.* No! You're not fuckin' doing it!

Claude: Okay . . . fine . . . Get me some makeup!

Light change. Bright, early morning.

Mom: Sheldon! Get up! Did you drink last night? What happened to your eyes? Did you get into a fight? . . . Is that makeup? . . . You know, people used to do things like that to your father all the time?

High-School Sheldon: I'm not him! Don't compare me to him!!

Mom: He's your blood, your father. You even have his hands. You can't deny that. No, you are not him . . . but when you get drunk and lose all control like that, you're handling yourself just like him.

Light change. Sound: club, audience noise. Sheldon moves left to mic, picks up guitar and plays.

SONG: TONTO'S LONE WORLD

I've always been in love with the Lone Ranger
Riding by his side, all my heart felt was pain
He was such a kind man. He would risk his life for anyone
It used to turn me on when he'd shoot his . . . gun
His big gun . . .

I've always wanted to be more than just his sidekick Tonto
I remember those gunfights, he'd say, "Tonto, get down"
One night he came to my teepee, sucked my pipe and had
   a little fun
We fell asleep in each other's arms when we were done
Yeah, done.

CHORUS ONE:

He was straight, but all it took was a six-pack of beer
If I was someone else would he give me his heart?
Silver, that dumb horse, should be hunted for game

I wish the Lone Ranger could just learn to love me
I loved it when he'd ride with me and hold my saddle horn
He must have known Indians ride bareback
The day came when he left me, he found out "kemosabe"
Really means "bend down," he got on his horse
And ran out of town, yeah, town! Yeah!

CHORUS TWO:

After he left me my whole life changed gears
The ratings fell, the TV show fell apart
I don't care if I still have fortune and fame
I just wish the Lone Ranger could just learn to love me

Sound of applause. Light change. Moves to centre.

PHONE FIGHT

Sheldon: The last fight my parents had before my mom left my dad. I was about ten. My mom says:

Mom: Sheldon, your dad knows I got paid today, so he's going to be coming here tonight. Here's the phone number to the police. I'm gonna put it on the coffee table, and if he shows up, you call it right away.

Sheldon: He showed up like she said he would. *Mimes this.* He kicked the door down, right off its hinges, and ripped the phone out of the wall.

Sonny: *Grabs Mom by the collar, and slaps her.* Where in the hell's the money?!

Mom: Hit me again, you cunt.

Young Sheldon: I grabbed Derek and ran into the bathroom and locked the door . . . I'm a chicken . . . .THE PHONE NUMBER! *Unlocks the door and tries to sneak by them.*

Mom: *Still struggling.* Sheldon, call the police quick!

Sonny: *Slaps her again, taking her to the floor. Pointing out into the audience, at Young Sheldon.* Sheldon! You touch that phone, I'll kill you.

Young Sheldon: *Mimes this.* I locked the door, kept Derek inside, went and got the phone number. They're on the floor of the doorway, their legs flailing, and I had to jump over top of them. I ran down the gravel road, barefooted, to our landlord's. I looked back. In the window, I could see my Dad digging in Mom's purse.

Sheldon: It would be the last time I saw him for years.

Light change. Sheldon moves right.

DEAR DAD:

Young Sheldon: *About ten years old.*

Dear Dad,
    I'm in Grimshaw now. I'm staying at Auntie Carol's while Mom is in the hospital and Derek is at Auntie Dolly's. I'm going to Holy Family School, and I'm in grade three. I go to church now with my best friend David, but I can't take the bread like he does. Mom says we're not coming back to Grande Prairie, and that you're not allowed to see us. She says that we're staying away for good. That's okay with me because I don't think you love us any more. You said you would kill me if I tried to phone the police for help. You even threw the radio at the puppy. I don't like it when you drink, Dad. You are mean to Mom, and mean to Derek. I still hope we get to see you, and I hope you are not mad at me and Derek for going away.
    Love,
    Sheldon

Light change. Moves back to centre.

THE MEANDER RIVER MEDICINE MAN

Sheldon: When I was thirteen, and in grade seven, I got very sick. *Sits in chair.* That hockey season, I was in atoms, and I was having a lot of problems with my feet. Every time I would take my skates off, that pain you generally feel, was becoming excruciating. *Begins to take skates off. The pain is intense. When he is finally finished—*

Mom: I want to take you to a specialist, and get you some of those expensive arch supports. It's because you've got ban-nock feet, flat like Indian bread. Your body's just changing. These are just growing pains. But this neck and back pain, I want you to go to the doctor and get it checked out.

Doctor One: *South African accent.* Well, Sheldon, I don't see any problems. I think you should start doing push-ups. They will strengthen your back. Do some for me right now. *Filling out a prescription.* I want you to take some ibuprofen, keep doing push-ups, stretch, and come back if it gets worse.

Sheldon: Later that week I had a terrible dream. *Suddenly is having trouble breathing.* My grandma's trailer was on fire, and she was trapped inside with my auntie Marilyn and my uncle Doug.

Sound: weird, dream music, sounds of a crackling fire can be heard. Lights change to fire-like dream.

I watched helplessly because I couldn't reach them because of the flames. Then suddenly, like a mirror in front of me, I could see my own face. It was red and puffy-eyed with tears. I tried to call out for help, but nothing could come out. I looked up and saw an eagle circling overhead. It swooped down, landing on a fence. As I moved toward it . . . *Sound ends with loud, eagle screeching . . .* and I woke up. I was in so much pain, my step-dad had to carry me upstairs. I told him about my dream. He went to the tele-phone and called a family friend from the Duncan Reserve just outside of town. He was a big old Indian.

Old Indian: *Slowly sits. rez accent.* I think this eagle in your dream is The Creator's way of trying to tell you someone is using bad medicine on your family. It starts with the parents, then moves to the next strongest in the family. Bring me Sheldon's shoes. *Someone hands him Sheldon's shoes. He inspects one shoe, finds nothing, sets it down, and then inspects the other, and finds something attached to the tongue. He holds both shoes up for Henry.* Henry, take these outside and burn them.

Sheldon: That night, I slept like a baby. Over the next couple of days, no one mentioned much of the ordeal, *mimes drying dishes,* until one day after supper doing dishes . . .

As he reaches up to put the dish away, he feels a sharp pain in his neck.

Mom: Sheldon, please, let's go to the hospital.

Sheldon: Not long in the Emergency Room I began convulsing. *Sits down in the chair and mimes:* My stomach muscles are rhythmically flexing, and getting painfully exhausted. *Suddenly drugged, and stoned, the convulsing slows, and is less intense.* After some Demerol, blood tests, X-rays, I overheard the doctors:

Doctor One: I want to send him to the University Hospital in Edmonton immediately. *To Mom.* You can ride in the jet with him, if you like.

Young Sheldon: *Still convulsing.* Don't worry, Mom. It's funny, . . . like The Exorcist.

Sheldon: I don't remember much of my first jet-ride, because they gave me more drugs. The next thing I remember was two doctors who gave me a small blue pill that looked like a Tiny Tart. It instantly dissolved under my tongue, leaving a nasty chemical taste. *Stoned.* Then the curtains in the emergency room began to rain flowers.

Doctor Two: *White male, mid-forties. Hands Sheldon a pillow, and helps him on to the chair.* Sheldon, we want you to just hang onto this pillow and slouch over. We're going to be giving you a spinal tap, which means we'll be drawing fluid from your spinal column to examine it. *Sterilizes Sheldon's back, and prepares needle.* First we will freeze your back. . . A little poke . . . We're going to start drawing fluid now . . . You're going to feel a lot of . . . pressure . . . on your lower back.

Sheldon: *Sits, hugging the back of the chair.* Then something like my life or my essence was being sucked from my lower back. I awoke in a hospital bed with no sense of time. I heard voices, . . . my Mom's . . . and . . . Sonny's, my biological father.

Sonny: *Crying, drunk.* My boy. My boy. Don't get up. Don't worry, my boy, they can fix broken backs.

Mom: Don't tell him that. Shel, your back's not broken. Your dad just wanted to see you. Now you've seen him, so get out. Leave.

Sheldon: I spent the next three weeks in a wheelchair in the U of A hospital. I went to school in the hospital to keep up, and celebrated Easter with the nurses. I had track marks on both my arms from blood tests. I had an EEG, a CAT scan, and an MRI. Nineteen doctors and two specialists reviewed my case.

Doctor Two: *Sits in chair.* Sheldon has large amounts of inflammation in his neck and back. We believe it is this inflammation that is putting pressure on his spinal chord, and is most likely triggering his convulsions. *Filling out a prescription.* I'm going to prescribe some more anti-inflammatories and more of those wonderful little blue pills if the convulsions reoccur. I'm going to put you on a vigorous, physical rehabilitation program, and you'll be back playing sports in no time.

Sheldon: I was so excited to be back with my family and friends, and I couldn't wait to be back at school, but on my first day back . . . *He convulses in pain.* My step-dad, Henry, took my mom aside.

Henry: *Stands.* Pat, these convulsions aren't going to stop. Those damn doctors in Edmonton couldn't help him. I want to take him to see a Medicine Man in Meander River. He's an old family friend. Sheldon, is this okay?

Young Sheldon: *Still convulsing.* O . . . okay, Dad.

Sheldon: We arrived in Meander River, and pulled in the driveway of a small, run-down house. At the door, my step-dad produced a brown paper bag with an offering of tobacco, food, and a little money inside. He immediately offered it to the old Indian man who answered the door, who made a brief, and vain attempt to turn it away. *Becomes hunched, very old, Medicine Man, still narrating.* He led us inside and went to a drawer, and got a bottle of what I think was holy water.

Medicine Man miming, pulls out a bottle from the drawer, opens it, dabs on his finger and does the sign of the cross three times while muttering a prayer in Cree. Then he pours some on Young Sheldon's head.

Medicine Man: *Thick Cree accent, and his English is not very good.* Where do you hurt? Where do you hurt?

Young Sheldon: *Sitting in chair.* In my neck, and my legs.

Sheldon: Then suddenly the old man started sucking on my neck. I looked to my step-dad for reassurance, and just about burst into uncomfortable laughter. My step-dad sat quietly, not watching. I started to feel sick. Then the nausea began to fade. Then the old man spit a large stone, shaped like a kidney bean, into a tissue.

Medicine Man: *Standing.* Where else? Where else?

Sheldon: *Sitting, eyes follow the Medicine Man who kneels in front of him.* Then he started sucking on the inside of my knee. Again, I wanted to laugh. I couldn't help it. Then I felt a surge of nausea and he spit a long, jagged rock into a tissue, and placed it near the other wad on the coffee table. He repeated the sucking on the other leg and produced another long jagged rock.

Medicine Man: *Still sitting, hunched.* These are spirits that hurting you. I put them in jar, bury in ground 'til morning. Then I make fire ceremony and burn them so they never hurt you again. I know who's hurting you, but I will not tell. Henry, where do you hurt?

Sheldon: Then he sucked on my step-dad's wrist, and spit another long jagged rock into a tissue. They had coffee after a while as I sat quietly, feeling strange. When we got home, I slept for fifteen hours straight, . . . and I never saw a doctor about it again. . . . Weird, huh?

Light change.

DAD'S FUNERAL

Sheldon: My half-sister Colette, and my half-brother Kevin took care of most of the funeral arrangements for my father. He was to be buried at Alexander Reserve where they lived. Marc, the hypnotist, gave me an advance on my cheque to help me get by, and I took a week off for the funeral, spending time with my family. But I didn't once, REALLY feel like crying. I was getting ready to go out on tour. During the wake, someone noticed my father had a metal belt-buckle on. My half-brother Kevin was upset.

Kevin: *Sobbing, sits in chair.* I fucked up, Shel. That gold and silver belt-buckle we got him . . . ? With the chief's head on it? The Elders are saying we shouldn't bury him with any metal, or it will weigh down his spirit. His hands . . . His hands are brittle. They're folded over it, and if we try to take it off him, we might break his hands. I fucked up, Shel.

Young Man Sheldon: *Moves behind chair, comforting him.* Shhhh. It's gonna be okay Kev. Just calm down. Breathe. Relax . . . Feel yourself becoming heavy and tired, rested and relaxed. . . .

Light change as he moves left to mic, and suddenly is Marc performing hypnosis.

Marc Savard: . . . Just let go of all tension. Take a nice, big, deep breath, and . . . SLEEP DEEP. *Snaps his fingers, light change as he moves back to centre.*

Young Man Sheldon: Marc, when you do that instant induction, how do you put people under so fast?

Marc Savard: Well, "under" isn't the right word, Sheldon. People are never "under," like under a spell. They are "in" a state of hypnosis. I'm going to tell you a secret. I don't do anything different than the long, "Your eyes are getting heavy, tired . . . " I simply say, "I'm going to hypnotize your friends in just a few seconds." Then all I have to do is pick the one who will be hypnotized easily. I have signs I look for. It all depends on that first one. If they drop like a sack of hammers, what do you think the next guy is thinking? "Holy shit, I'm next!" Right? Remember this: What's expected tends to be realized. You know what? I'm going to stop introducing you as "an amateur comedian." If people expect you're an amateur, they'll treat you like one.

Sheldon: We toured schools, communities, bars, clubs, comedy cabarets through BC, Alberta, a bit of Saskatchewan.

Blackout. Sound: Comedy Club Intro # 2.

Announcer Voice: Ladies and Gentlemen, please put your hands together for the comedy of Sheldon Elter!

Sheldon the Comedian: *Spotlight up, as Sheldon moves to the mic.* Hello, my name is Sheldon Elter, and I will be your Native comedian for this evening. I know I don't look that Native. My skin's not that dark. I don't have the long braids . . . and I'm working.

You know, people don't have to be close to us to understand who we are. I mean, for the White man, the name John Smith, tells you nothing about John Smith. For us Indians, our names reflect who we are. Like Johnny Runs Like the Wind . . . He's very fast. Or Billy Buffalo Head . . . Well, he's got a big head. Or Shirley Big Canoe . . . Okay, that's a bad example. There was my ex-girlfriend, Tammy The Stupid Bitch Who Takes All Your Money And Uses It To Play Bingo And When The Money's All Gone The Slut Leaves You For Another Guy. We broke up. Now she's with my cousin, Ernie Double-Crossing Prick. That's why it's important when you're dating to pay attention to the names. I think that's why Shirley Big Canoe was always after my brother, Derek Drags in the Dirt.

Puberty was a very hard time for me. My brother, Will Tomahawk Whacker, was very helpful to me during that time. He even bought me my first wet-dream catcher. I was so inspired, that I wrote a song. *Picks up guitar and plays.*

SONG: SELF-LOVE

They say for every guy today
Kleenex is used in another way
Like it is going out of style
Victoria's Secret, Playboy too
For older people
Sears helped you
On those cold and lonely Friday nights
Self-Love, self-love
A magazine and a bottle of lotion
Self-love, self-love
Just like the guitar motion

Slides hand up and down guitar neck.

I've got a grip on reality

I took my own virginity
At the tender age of thirteen
No STDs and no miracle potions
Self-love, Self-love
Just like the guitar— *Slides hand up and down guitar neck, climaxes, and grunts.* —motion.

Sound: of applause. Light change as he moves to centre.

WOODSTOCK '99

Sheldon: That summer, I went to Woodstock '99.

Sound: of concert music and crowd noise.

American Dude: Don't worry about the upside down flag with the anarchy symbol. The police already came by and told my uncle that people can't camp here. If any cops ask, it's a peace rally.

Dealer Dude: Get your friendly bud here. Maui Wowi! White Rhino!

Dealer Dude Two: Ecstasy! Mushrooms! Doses, doses, doses!

Young Man Sheldon: What's a dose, man?

Dealer Dude Two: Acid, man . . . Here, I'll sell you a half-sheet for fifty bucks.

Young Man Sheldon: Sure . . . *To audience.* I don't even know what half a sheet is . . . FIFTY TABS OF ACID!!! OH, MY GOD!! IT'S GEORGE CLINTON!! HE'S RIGHT THERE, MAN!! *Singing.* "We want the funk! Gotta have that—" Who's touching me??? Holy shit, that guy is fucking that chick while she's hanging on to me . . . Let's do some ecstasy. *Very stoned, melts to the floor.*

Rave Girl: *On her knees.* Is this your first time . . . Awww. Do you want a hug?

Sheldon: The rest is pretty much a blur. I came back to Canada with a heavy drug habit. After some flashbacks— *Swats at something that isn't there.* —and rest, I did one last comedy performance, and I was off to Grant MacEwan College's Theatre Arts Program.

The storytelling quality of *Métis Mutt* emphasized the transformative
power of the performer with minimual use of set or costume.

PHOTOGRAPH COURTESY OF DAVID WILLIAMSON

Student Sheldon: *Trying to do yoga stance.* It's my third day. I'm in this weird movement class. I don't know anything about this hippie shit. Then my body began to shake and vibrate. *He shakes and vibrates, approaches teacher.* I feel really strange, . . . kind of angsty, like I'm gonna cry. Is that normal?

Teacher: You feel like you need to cry? . . . That's okay. You go and cry somewhere. I'll tell your next teacher you can't make it to class. It'll be all right.

Student Sheldon: *About to cry.* I need to find some place quick. I'm gonna start and everyone is watching. I found a stairwell, and hid underneath the stairs. *Crouches in a fetal position, centre stage.* I felt like a pressure cooker about to explode. Then the pressure would move up into my throat, then my face would try to stop it, *His face quivers, about to cry.*

Sheldon: The dam was broken, and I couldn't stop. I cried for an hour, non-stop. I didn't like it, because I thought I wouldn't be able to stop, and I didn't know why. As the term went by, the training got more difficult, emotionally and physically demanding, and . . . I found myself having these strong feelings bubbling up to the surface. I began to do whatever I could to suppress them. I went to raves. My first ecstasy trip was awesome, and then I'd do two hits at once, and soon I was up to four or five a night. When I couldn't score "E", I took Tylenol, NyQuil, Neo Citran, ANYTHING that could dull my senses or get me high. I started cutting myself, using a razor blade.

Sheldon sits on chair, lifts his shirt. His breathing is short and fast. He mimes cutting his stomach. It is as though the cuts allow him to breathe normally again.

Sheldon: *Still sitting, on the phone, crying.* Hi, Marc. I'm sorry to call so late. I didn't know who else to call. . . . I didn't want to call anyone else. I'm going crazy, man. Twila wants me back. I said no, then she quits school, her mom calls me for help . . . I dropped out of theatre school . . . I'm doing a lot of drugs . . . I'm cutting myself . . . I want to kill myself.

Marc Savard: *On the phone.* Okay, Sheldon, I'm coming to town soon. Let's meet, okay? *Then, face to face.* Sheldon, you want to know what I think? I can offer my services as a hypnotist. We could do some clinical hypnotherapy if you want, but that's not what I think you need. Ultimately, you are just going to realize that it's YOU, YOU who wants to change, and that you always have had the power to do it. I want you to come back on tour with me. You're telling me how you don't know what it is you're doing at this musical theatre school, that you don't like it. People still ask if the comedian is coming back when they book shows with us. You know you can't drink, smoke, or do drugs on my time. Just come, and write some new stuff, explore yourself, and do what you do best.

Sheldon the Comedian: *Turns to Marc, jotting down notes.* Marc? I need an idea for a song that has nothing to do with Indians.

Marc Savard: *Driving tour bus, thinks for a moment* . . . Self-love.

Sheldon the Comedian smiles, then quickly writes something down.

Sheldon the Comedian: *Stands.* Marc! Johnny "Bagpipes" Johnston wants me to do a five-minute spot before his opener, TOMORROW NIGHT!!!

Johnny Bagpipes: *Sitting, slightly drunk.* I think you're funny, kid. But this character, "The Chief", with the braided wig, drop it. People come to a comedy club to see comedians. If they want to see an actor, they'll go to a theatre. YOU are funny. Just be yourself.

Sheldon: *Standing.* Marc? Can I talk to you for a second? I just wanted to tell you that you have been a great boss. No. You have been more than that. You have been a great friend, like a big brother. That's why I have to be honest with you. I don't want to be a comedian. I am sorry if I mislead you. I just wanted to impress you. Show you that I could do it. I wanted to impress my family too. They are so proud of what I am doing. I can't lie to myself anymore, or run from the challenges that come from what you really want in life. I want to be an actor. I want to go back to school, and I want to graduate. *Does yoga stance as seen before.* So I went back to theatre school, and I was kickin' ass! I got better grades than I ever had before, and I graduated.

Sheldon: The last time I saw my father alive, I was in grade eleven. My brother couldn't come with me to see him, so I asked my cousin Kenny, we all call him "Trouble," to come with me. My Dad was living in a nine-foot trailer.

Nervous, Sheldon knocks on the door. Then, Sonny opens the door, looks at both of the boys, confused.

Sheldon: My Dad couldn't tell which one of us was his son.

Trouble: Uncle Sonny, it's me. Kenny. Trouble? Shel, I'll just go wait in the car.

Sheldon: Dad told me how excited he was to be coming to see me graduate. We laughed at old times, and we played the guitar. He didn't even know I played. He showed me one riff.

Grabbing the guitar, Sonny sits back down in the chair, and plays the riff we hear at the end of "I Like the Booze". Then Sheldon tries, unsuccessfully. Sonny puts the guitar away, and mimes a valued box with photographs, and documents, and returns to the chair to show Sheldon.

Sonny: D'you remember this? That's when I took you and Derek and you rode on them ponies? And this one's from when we went to Lac Ste. Anne. These are my papers. See there? The Michelle Band. That's where I'm from. I woulda never got these without your Mom's help. She got them for me. I don't know anything about that stuff.

Sheldon: After about an hour, it was time to leave.

Young Man Sheldon: Well, Dad, I'll see ya. Take care. I'll make sure and tell Derek when he can come and see you. We'll phone you.

Sonny: Well, we'll see you, my boy. *Reaches into his pocket.* D'you need any money for gas? . . . Okay, well you kids drive safe, and you call me when you get in. *He embraces his son awkwardly.*

Sheldon: On January 1st, 1999, my father, Robert "Sonny" L'hirondelle, died. Some might say "God took him." Standing by his body, I got to tell him how I felt without him being drunk or interrupting me because he didn't want to hear it. *Moves right, warm amber light.*

Sheldon's Funeral Oration: First of all, Dad, I love you, and I forgive you for all the things you've done to us. I don't blame you for any of my drinking, or drug problems. It's not Mom's fault that I grew up too fast. I could have chosen to be like any other kid. But instead, I chose to try to be a father to my little brother, but I wasn't, . . . and I couldn't. You can only take responsibility for yourself. I am sorry for all the times I said I hate you, because I don't. I am my own person. I have grown up without you, and I'm a man now.

Light fades, Sound: Comedy Club Intro # 2.

Announcer Voice: Ladies and Gentlemen, please put your hands together for the comedy of Sheldon Elter!

Comedian spotlight as Sheldon moves to mic.

COMEDY BREAKDOWN

Sheldon: Hello, my name is Sheldon Elter—and it is not just my stage name. It's the only name I have. I have one father, and one step-dad. My mom never told me to tell a joke about a bunch of fathers I don't have. Why would she? I do look Native. I have high cheek-bones, and an Indian nose. I like the way I look, and so does my White girlfriend. I'm not the only Indian working. I know many Indians who work, and many who work harder than me. I know many Indians who do not like bingo. I never had a Ford F150 when I was sixteen, and I don't know any Indians who were just given one. Some Indians do get certain advantages, living on the reserve, but I don't live on one. I have known Indians who stole bikes, but when you compare it to what got stolen from them. . . . I've never been in a room with forty squaws, or Native women, but it sounds like a pretty good party to me. A Native woman on birth control is probably a responsible decision. Many thousands of native North Americans were winked at like this, *gesture of aiming gun* at the massacre at Wounded Knee, at the massacre on the Milk River, at Batoche. When

I go out, I get winked at sometimes, and it feels good. My dad wasn't buried in a garbage can, he had a beautiful casket, with six pallbearers. But he did have a tragically hard, bitter, self-destructive, and short life. I intend to do better.

Picks up guitar and plays.

SONG: PRETTY FLY FOR A RED GUY

You know it's kind of hard to be an Indian today
That hair isn't cool, but he braids it anyway
With a hat and rubber boots he thinks he's in style
He's not a Cowboy, he's an Indian in denial

When I'm on the street, cops suspect me first
It always is the same, I must be bloody cursed
Assimilation's a joke, we'll create our own fate
And celebrate in the teepee, smokin' pipe and hallucinate
The world needs one of these, so hey, hey
Do this Indian's thing:

Give it to me baby, *Like war cry* wah-wah!
Give it to me baby, wah-wah!
Give it to me baby, wah-wah!

And all the girlies say I'm pretty fly for a red guy

Blackout

Casey (Jimmy Hodges) speaks to a video camera in
Code Word: Time. The image behind is a live feed.

PHOTOGRAPH COURTESY OF DAVID WILLIAMSON

Code Word: Time

Leah Simone Bowen

INTRODUCTION

This play is subversive. The first time I read *Code Word: Time* I was tricked into a sense of sitcom safety. After about ten pages, I spread out on the couch and set my expectation dial to fluff. Everything is nice. Nobody gets hurt. Sanitized versions of tender tunes by The Beatles accompany vocabulary-expanding games played for the grand prize of a pickle. A cuddly security guard plays make-believe with his video camera while his worship of John Ritter is echoed by a zany alternative version of *Three's Company* set in an elevator—all so pre-adolescent, cute, and harmless—like a children's cartoon set in an octopus' garden. I idly made note of a couple of events in the script that didn't seem right. I thought they were typos, orphans that slipped between the drafts. I attributed it to sloppy writing and kept on traipsing down a path lined by marshmallow trees . . . then Maxwell's silver hammer came down on my head.

I stopped reading and went back to the beginning because I was stunned. I did not know what was happening. I was horrified and I still maintain that *Code Word: Time* is best understood as a work of horror. By that I do not mean just the shock of the unexpected that comes when the "code word" is revealed (and a successful production of the script will keep the title's meaning hidden until that "time"), but I am also referring to the vision of the play that speaks to this particular moment in history. *Code Word: Time* is a horrific vision of our culture's ubiquitous surveillance technology combined with a seemingly limitless hunger for celebrity, violence, and misogyny. The play presents our culture as fundamentally immoral and that vision is backed up by the reality of "Reality TV", the Internet's niches of dark human behaviour, and our compliant daily acceptance of corruption.

After I finished reading the play, I stood up, placed the script on my kitchen table, and applauded the sheaf of paper before me. When Leah and her director / collaborator Ottillie Parfitt came to call, I had very little interest in sitting down with the script and sharing my penciled notes with them. Eventually I did share those notes with them but clearly they knew what they were doing and I was itching to know how they saw the play working in the theatre.

The Nextfest production made substantial use of a digital projector and live camera feeds. It often created a dislocating effect of simultaneously observing an actor talk to a video camera in the foreground AND having that video camera's live capture of the actor being projected behind as a two-dimensional background. The audience found itself having to choose which media was more compelling: the life-sized or the magnified. While the production elements were quite elaborate, some of Ottillie and Leah's original schemes that did not come to fruition were even more so: including putting Casey's janitorial station in my office and doing a live feed from a location hidden from the audience. In the end we had Casey's station on stage right, the elevator stage left, with projections on one large screen upstage of the action.

Because the Roxy Theatre was built as a cinema, projections work remarkably well and we have found that every time we combine large projections over live actors, the effect is stunning. What we have also found is that movies (no matter how low-tech you go, even if it's a live feed) are monsters. They are time consuming, inflexible, and dependent upon inconsistent and unreliable factors. However, they can also do things with time and space that typical theatre tricks cannot. If you wish to produce this play (or any other play that can benefit from multimedia tricks such as the next play in this volume, *Beneath The Deep Blue Sky*). I urge you not to underestimate the pre-production demands ahead of you. If anything, overestimate . . . and then double it.

– S.P.

PRODUCTION HISTORY

Code Word: Time was first presented at NeXtFest 2001 at the Roxy Theatre with the following team:

Casey: *Jimmy Hodges*
Lucy: *Leah Simone Bowen*
Turrin: *Jesse Gervais*
Joel: *Morgan Jones*
Director: *Ottillie Parfitt*
Stage Manager: *Kate Mahoney*
Designer: *Wojtek Koslinski*
Videographer: *Sophie Morgadinho*
Dramaturg: *Elyne Quan*

The play was then presented at the 2002 Edmonton Fringe with the following team:

Casey: *Jimmy Hodges*
Lucy: *Kattina Michele*
Turrin: *Murray Utas*
Joel: *Kevin Gillese*
Director: *Ottillie Parfitt*
Stage Manager: *Kerri Gibson-Loranger*
Designer: *Mateusz Odrobny*
Video Director: *Sophie Morgadinho*
Cinematographer: *Dave Luxton*

THE CHARACTERS

Casey Ginter: Caretaker. Seemingly dim-witted guy, loves being underestimated.
Lucy Williams: Shy, awkward and unaware waste Management Director.
Turrin: Charismatic and aloof.
Joel: The loveable Parking Ticket Officer.

THE SETTING

An elevator and the caretaker's office in a downtown office tower.

PRODUCTION NOTES

The opening stage directions mostly reflect the technical solutions used in the Fringe production. The Nextfest production did not have four televisions but instead used a video switcher to send different images through one digital projector. It is conceivable that one could tell the nut of this story without the assistance of any electrical appliances at all. However, the story of this play is prompted by technology and technical solutions should be employed if only to demonstrate that the technology in the play is not speculative: the play depicts a world in which cameras are omnipresent and ordinary folk can generate content and broadcast it with relative ease. This should be reflected in the production values of the play.

Code Word: Time

An elevator sits at stage right. Its doors and walls are defined only by light. A small surveillance camera hangs over the elevator. Two desks on a riser sit at stage left. The front desk, closest to the audience, is cluttered with old videotapes, DVDs and papers. The back desk, which is facing the audience, holds three televisions. On the first TV (TV1) is a live feed of the three characters trapped in the elevator. The second TV (TV2) is Casey's personal screen, which he watches when he videotapes himself. The third TV (TV3) will show clips of Three's Company episodes and anything else Casey wants to watch. The TVs can be substituted with screens.

SCENE ONE

As lights come up on Casey, "Eleanor Rigby" plays in the background. His back is to the audience. On TV3 he is watching an episode of Three's Company. He sets up his camera; satisfied that his face is centred in the screen he begins talking. Every now and then he stutters.

Casey: Perception, that's my problem. Well, I think it's everyone's problem. You know what I'm talking about. Why do so many of us dodge our high-school reunions and hide when we see a familiar face coming around the corner? Well, 'cause we change. Who wants to be remembered for the person you used to be when you were young and stupid. For instance, up until I was thirteen I used to stutter really bad. I remember during a spelling bee I spent forever trying to pronounce the word 'conglomerate'. There I was for ten excruciating minutes. I stood there saying, "cccccccccconggggggggggggg." It was horrible. Lucky for me, my family moved around a lot and we left shortly after. But each place presented a new problem. At my new school, I developed a severe intestinal problem. See—I had uncontrollable gas. I had no choice but to stay at home. If I didn't, I risked offending a lot of people. My Dad disagreed with me and forced me out of the house each morning. I was ostracized and I can't say I really blamed them, especially in gym class. But now I'm working here, and believe you me, I'm enjoying myself. Nobody expects too much from me and that's okay. I don't feel as stuck anymore . . . well, maybe a little. . . . But, that's okay. I love being underestimated.

SCENE TWO

Total darkness. We cannot see Lucy, Turrin, or Joel. They have recently gotten stuck in the elevator on the fourteenth of twenty floors. The power has gone out. We will hear a match trying to be lit, with no luck and then success. We see Joel holding the flame to his face, smiling, he laughs and snuffs out the flame in the process. He tries again, this time burning his fingers.

Joel: *Still in the dark.* I've run out of matches. *Silence.* Does anyone have a match or maybe a lighter?

Silence.

Turrin: Are you cold?

Joel: Pardon me?

Turrin: Are you cold?

Joel: No. . . Not really.

Turrin: Then why do you need a match?

Joel: It's dark in here and I thought that if we could see we could . . .

Turrin: We could what?

Joel: Well, I don't know I just wanted a match.

Rustling.

Lucy: Here. *She produces a match, lights it and gives him the box. The match burns to her fingers.* Ouch!

Joel tries to light a bunch of matches. He lights some, but most are snuffed out during this conversation.

Joel: Oh, watch it! I already burnt myself.

Lucy: Here let me try, there . . . oh. *Another match goes out.*

Joel: Forget it. I'm actually not minding it. It's kind of interesting having a conversation in the dark. It's like a confessional, you can't see who you're talking to, therefore you feel more open to—

Turrin interrupts him abruptly by flicking open his Zippo lighter and giving it to Joel. Silence.

SCENE THREE

Casey is still talking into his camera. Three's Company is on TV3. The elevator version of "A Hard Day's Night" plays.

Casey: Jeeze, I'm excited. . . . No, not what you're thinking, not like that. I'm excited because I think I've figured it all out. I used to find myself waiting for things a lot. I used to wait for cabs and buses, then I thought I got smart and started car-pooling but I still had to wait. I wait in lines. I wait on the phone a lot. I've waited for women, they never wait back. It also seems to me that I wait a lot for food. In restaurants or at home—the macaroni has to cook. I waited in school for help, waited for my parents, waited for my first kiss. But now I'm not waiting any more. I have a plan: get a car, get a microwave, get a girl, get smart . . . See, my plan is to turn on, turn up, and tune out, that's what they say and that's what I plan to do. . . .

The emergency alarm from the elevator starts to ring. Casey, startled, starts to look through the papers on his desk The ringing continues. Turrin is speaking and his voice is heard through a speaker on Casey's desk.

Turrin: Hello? Hello?

Casey: Hello, maintenance.

Turrin: Hi, we've been trapped in here for quite some time.

Silence.

Turrin: Hello? We're trapped!

Casey: Hello?

Turrin: Can you hear us? We are trapped in elevator number two, I think we're on the fourteenth floor. . . .

Casey: All right then, I'll get you out in a jiff.

Turrin: Thank you. How long do you think that will take?

Silence.

Turrin: Hello . . .

Joel: Listen, the lights have gone out. Can you do anything about that? It's really dark in here.

Casey: I hear you. *With a flick of a switch the lights go on, and the alarm goes off. Casey turns on his monitor (TV1) and we can see the three of them on the screen. Casey speaks to the screen.*

Turrin: Thank you. About how long do you think this will take? See, I have to contact some people. I'm going to be late.

Casey: Oh that's too bad. I'm working as fast as I can, but you'd probably be best to call someone and let them know what the situation is.

Turrin: I can't call them I don't have my cellphone.

Casey: How many people are in there?

Turrin: Three: two, and myself.

Casey: So four, three people plus you equals four.

Turrin: No, there are three of us. Just three.

Casey: Why don't you call one of them and see if they have a phone?

Turrin: They're in here with me. There are three people trapped in this elevator.

Casey: Right, and what I'm asking is, does one of them have access to a phone?

Turrin: Look, do you think I would be asking you to phone people, if I had access to a phone?

Silence.

Turrin: HELLO! Jesus Christ, this guy is an idiot!

Lucy: Hello?

Casey: Hi there.

Lucy: Hi, is there an emergency exit in the roof or anything that we should know about?

Casey: No that's an old elevator you're standing in. The only way out is for me to pry the doors open.

Lucy: Well. How long do you estimate this will take?

Casey: Like I said, this is an old elevator, I have to get the right tools.

Lucy: I understand that but, is there anyone you could—

Casey: Who's talking?

Lucy: Lucy, my name is Lucy Williams.

Casey: Lucy! It's me Casey.

Lucy: Casey?

Casey: Casey Ginter, I'm in maintenance, I fixed that leak over your desk a couple of months ago.

Lucy: Oh . . . okay . . .

Casey: How are you?

Lucy: Well, I'd be better if I could get out of here . . . Look Casey, can you work as fast as you can, we're all in a hurry . . . okay? Hello?

Joel: He's not answering, he probably left to get us out . . . Well, since we're going to be here for a while longer, I'm going to sit down. Hi, I'm Joel.

Joel sits on the floor and looks up at Lucy. It looks as though he is trying to look up her skirt and she quickly sits down. He sticks his hand out to offer a handshake. She has her hands full with a bag/briefcase. She awkwardly tries to get her stuff out of the way so she can shake his hand. There is a pause while Joel keeps his hand out for her. She finally grabs his hand.

Lucy: Hi.

Joel: *To Turrin.* I'm Joel.

Turrin: Hello.

Joel: and you are?

Turrin: Turrin.

Joel: Turning?

Turrin: Tur-rin.

Joel: As in the shroud? Oh, that's cool. Well, Turrin why don't you join us down here, since were going to be here for a bit. Why not get comfortable?

Turrin: I'm fine.

Joel: Okay. So Turrin what is it that you do? I see you have a briefcase with you. . . .

Turrin: It's really none of your business.

Silence.

Joel: Does anyone have the time?

Lucy: Sorry, I don't have a watch on me.

Joel: Turning?

Turrin: Sorry?

Silence.

Joel: So, do you usually work on the weekend?

Lucy: Sometimes.

Joel: I have to pick up some keys from a friend.

Turrin stares at Joel.

Joel: It is cold in here . . . anybody cold?

Pause.

Joel: So, Lisa.

Lucy: Lucy.

Joel: Pardon me?

Lucy: Lucy, my name is Lucy.

Silence.

Joel: So, Lucy what do you do? Do you work in this building?

Lucy: Yes, I work on the top floor in the waste management section.

Joel: Waste management . . . cool . . . What exactly do you do in, uh, waste management?

Lucy: I process statistics on waste, mostly glass.

Joel: So how much glass do we waste?

Lucy: A lot.

Joel: Oh right, do you teach people the three R's, reduce, reuse and recycle?

Lucy: No, I work in the office.

Silence.

Joel: Does anyone—

Lucy: *To Turrin.* Have we . . . Sorry I cut you off.

Joel: No, go ahead, what were you going to say?

Lucy: *To Turrin.* I know this might sound like a line, it's not, but do I know you from somewhere?

Turrin: I don't think so . . . what floor did you say you worked on?

Lucy: Top floor, in waste management.

Turrin: We've probably seen each other in the building before. I'm a consultant so I'm in and out all the time.

Lucy: Oh, who do you consult for? What section?

Turrin: . . . I'm a law consultant. I'm brought in when there are any—interruptions.

Lucy: What do you mean by interruptions? Wouldn't you be there to handle any lawsuits or explain bylaws or something?

Turrin: Exactly—interruptions.

Joel: That's really interesting, a lawyer. . . . So again, explain this to me. What kind of law do you practice? *Smiles.*

Turrin: What is it that you do?

Joel: I asked you first.

Turrin: I asked you second.

Joel: I work for the city.

Turrin: What do you do for the city?

Joel: I work in a special zoning division.

Turrin: Doing what exactly?

Joel: Well, I have several duties.

Turrin: Which are?

Joel: I'm in charge of issuing zoning infractions on stationary vehicles.

Turrin: I see, so in other words you write parking tickets.

Joel: Yeah . . . So?

Turrin: That's a very evil profession.

Joel: I just give out parking tickets.

Turrin: No, what you really do is confirm the fact to everyone that your fellow man is just lurking around the corner waiting to screw you over.

Joel: Hey man, I'm just trying to make a living like everyone else.

Turrin: Really? I have a question for you Joel.

Joel: Sure.

Turrin: Do you believe in karma?

Joel: I don't know? I guess. *Turrin kneels down beside him making him nervous.* Yes, I would say, I believe in karma.

Turrin: Good. *He grabs Joel's collar and punches him hard.*

TV2 turns on.

Turrin sits in prison. Close-up on his face. We hear an off-screen interviewer.

Interviewer: Were you violent as a child?

Extreme close-up on Turrin, he looks down with no emotion and no response.

Interviewer: Tell me about Joel.

Turrin stays in the same posture.

Interviewer: Did you know there were cameras in the elevator?

Turrin looks up—still no emotion.

Fade out.

SCENE FOUR

Casey sits watching an episode of Three's Company. It is a short scene which he has looped. The scene has Chrissie standing in between Jack and Janet. Chrissie is wearing a fur coat and as Jack tries to get her to take it off, Janet gets her to put it back on. The scene continues as the two circle around Chrissie, one taking off a sleeve of a jacket, and the other putting it back on. Casey sits laughing, and then, after watching it loop three times, rewinds it and presses pause. He turns writes something on a paper and then prepares himself and looks into the camera. "With a Little Help from My Friends" plays in the background.

Casey: I forgot to tell you, I just got my certificate from Lord's School of Hollywood Directing. This now means I am a real director. I have always been one, this just makes it official. My uncle Dean ran coffee for the one and only Leonard Nemoy. Most people think of Leonard Nemoy as Mr. Spock from Star Trek, but he's actually a brilliant and unrecognized director. He directed Three Men and a Baby, which became the number one movie in the world at the time. So anyway, Uncle Dean let me in on all the trade secrets when I was young and I have been applying them ever since. My first film at the institute was an experimental take on Titanic. I shot it completely in the dark and all you could hear for the first three hours was rain falling. It was brilliant. My teacher didn't fully appreciate what I was going for, but always remember that Walt Disney went bankrupt several times before building Disneyland. It's negative reactions that make me reach for my favourite book, *holding it up,* and one of the best books of the century, I might add, Chicken Soup For the Soul. I always read the "consider this" section. *He reads from the book.* "Consider this, Albert Einstein did not speak until he was four years old and didn't read until he was seven. His teacher described him as mentally slow, unsociable and adrift forever in his foolish dreams". I will remember these things for the future. I won't be mean to the naysayers. No I won't. I'll invite them in for some ladyfingers and Irish coffee and we'll watch the screening for my latest movie starring the late, great John Ritter. In my opinion John Ritter was the real Jim Carrey, he was the comedic genius of his generation. And he was meant to get the part on Three's Company if you ask me. I mean think about it. His name is John Ritter and his name on the show was Jack Tripper. John Ritter, Jack Tripper? John Ritter, Jack Tripper?

SCENE FIVE

The three in the elevator are all sitting down. Joel has his hand pressed into his eye.

Lucy: Maybe I should look at it?

Joel: I'm fine.

Turrin: Let her look at it.

Joel: Excuse me?

Lucy: I just want to look at it.

Joel: *To Turrin.* No, I'm sorry. I can't believe you're actually speaking to me. That words are actually coming out of your mouth and that they are directed at me is mind boggling since you just assaulted me.

Turrin: I got a little hot under the collar.

Joel: Really, well I'm sure we'll work all that out in court.

Lucy: Hold on for just a minute—now let me look at your eye. *He reveals that he has a cut over his eye.* Okay it's cut and it looks like it may need some stitches.

Joel: Wonderful.

Lucy: Let me look in my purse and see if I have a Band-Aid.

Joel: A Band-Aid?

Lucy: Well, I need to find something to hold it together for the time being. *She searches and finds stamps.* Okay, I'll have to use these.

Turrin: You're using stamps?

Lucy: They're the only things that I have that will close the cut. When we get out he can go get a bandage. I'll need you to turn to me.

Joel: This is humiliating.

They face each other and she starts to clean his face with a Kleenex. Joel smiles at her and she smiles back. She puts the stamps on his cut. They share a moment.

Joel: Thanks.

Lucy: No problem.

Silence.

Lucy: Do you think anyone's coming for us?

Joel: They have to. They can't just leave us in here.

Lucy: By now I'm not so sure.

We can see Joel and Turrin look as though they are getting hotter.

Joel: It's boiling in here. I'm taking this off. *He takes off his sweater.*

Turrin: It is quite hot. *He takes off his jacket.*

Pause. They both look at Lucy. She doesn't notice. They look at each other. Joel flinches and puts his hand up to his ear as though he has heard a loud noise.

Lucy: Is something wrong?

Joel: No, it's nothing. Don't you think it's hot in here?

Lucy: Not really.

Joel: Are you serious? I'm boiling. Maybe you should take your jacket off. You don't want to overheat in here. *Joel moves to take her jacket off. He gets one arm out and goes around to her other side to repeat the move as mirrored in the Three's Company episode.*

Lucy: Excuse me!

By this time Joel is already over to her other arm. Turrin rushes to put her jacket back on.

Turrin: What are you doing? She said she doesn't want to take it off!

The dance continues.

Lucy: I'm really not hot!

Joel: I just think that we might be here for a while. . . .

Turrin: Well, it's not your decision to make—

Lucy: Thank you, but I can make up my mind—

Joel: Don't be silly, I'm not trying to patronize you I just think . . .

Turrin: Leave her coat on!

They stop. Beat. Lucy takes off her coat.

Lucy: Well, maybe it is a little warm.

Joel and Turrin still facing forward, smile.

SCENE SIX

The elevator version of "Help!" plays in the background.

Casey: See, in life everything goes through changes, as did Three's Company. First there was Jack, Chrissie and Janet. Then Chrissie left to go back to the farm and her cousin Cindy came to replace her. Then she left and Terry the nurse moved in. Even though everything kept changing, everything stayed the same. There was always some misunderstanding, some crazy mix up that involved signals getting crossed, or someone missing the point and not paying attention to what was going on around them. Sometimes people on that show just walked around with blinders on, but I guess that's what made it a hit—the mystery of it all and of course Jack Tripper. . . .

(TV3) The camera is a silent interviewer. We see a crowd of people.

Cut to two female fans.

Female Fan 1: We love you Joel. WE LOVE YOU, YOU'RE SOO HOT! WHOOOO!

Female Fan 2: I just want Joel to know that I know he didn't mean it, and that even if he did . . . I LOVE YOU.

Fade out.

SCENE SEVEN

Joel sits in the elevator reading a Reader's Digest. Turrin paces back and forth. Lucy is filing her nails.

Joel: Does anyone have the time?

Lucy: I told you, I don't have the time.

Joel: It's just weird that nobody has the time.

Turrin: Joel.

He stops pacing for a second, looks at Joel and continues pacing again.

Lucy: Do you think you could stop pacing? It's kind of unnerving. Plus you don't have much room.

Turrin: I'm bored.

He continues pacing making the elevator bigger and bigger.

Joel: What are you doing?

Turrin: I'm pacing, that is what I'm doing. Pacing, haven't you seen anyone pace before? What are you doing?

Joel: Reading. You do know how to read don't you?

Turrin: Reader's Digest?

Joel: *Reader's Digest* is a good read. It has great articles, good jokes and I read it to increase my vocabulary. The word power section is really good. *He pulls a Reader's Digest out of his bag.* Let's do some word power. Here Lucy you quiz us. *She flips through to find it.* Page fifty-four.

Lucy: Okay, word power. *She reads.* "The following words ending in 'ology', Greek for the study of, have some similarity in sound, making it easy to confuse one with the other. Pick the answer that most closely defines the area of study." Ready? Number one: Archaeology is: A. ancient societies, B. rare birds, C. arches and columns, or D. myths?

Joel: Ancient societies.

Lucy: *She looks for the answer.* Correct, five points for you.

Turrin: You both do realize you're in an elevator playing word power don't you?

Joel: What else is there to do?

Lucy: Why don't you join in?

Turrin: No thanks.

Lucy: What if I make the game interesting?

Pause. Turrin and Joel exchange glances.

Turrin: Like how?

Lucy: Well, I have to confess—I have food in my purse.

Turrin: What? What do you have?

Lucy: A chocolate bar.

Turrin: You've had a chocolate bar this whole time and you didn't bother to tell us?

Lucy: I was saving it, for an emergency—anyway its up for grabs. Whoever wins gets to share it with me.

Joel: I'm in.

Turrin: All right I'm in. I'm starving so I'm in.

Joel: But, I thought you were allergic.

Lucy: You're allergic to chocolate?

Turrin: No . . . Let's play.

Lucy: Etymology is: A. butterflies, B. dinosaurs, C. origins, or D. ancient languages?

Joel: What was B?

Lucy: B was dinosaurs.

Turrin: Can you repeat the word?

Lucy: Etymology

Turrin: Etymology

Joel: How do you spell that?

Lucy: Joel, just guess.

Joel: I'm not guessing, I'm starving.

Turrin: Just spell it.

Lucy: E-T-Y-M-O-L-O-G-Y

Joel: E-T-I?

Lucy: No E-T-Y-M-O—

Turrin: Just guess!

Joel writes down his guess and gives it to her.

Lucy: The correct response is C. Joel you win.

~~**Joel:** Yes! Break out the chocolate!!!~~

~~*Lucy takes the chocolate bar out of her purse.*~~

Joel: Bite it in half. *She does and gives him his half.*

Joel: Cheers.

He looks at her flirtatiously and smiles. She smiles back and they eat.

~~**Joel:** You want to know something?~~

Lucy: What?

Joel: You're really pretty.

She is taken by surprise and smiles shyly. They look at each other.

Turrin: *Under his breath.* Oh god.

SCENE EIGHT

The elevator version of "I Should Have Known Better" plays.

Casey: They say imitation is the sincerest form of flattery. I truly believe that. All great works of art are just a regurgitation of someone else's idea or a reordering of one good idea. It's like when you start listening to a new band and you really like 'em 'cause they're all new and so you go out and buy another one of their CDs because you know that all their songs are going to be basically the same but sound different . . . well you don't know for sure, but you do, but you don't know that you know, like subliminal messages . . . the key to ripping off someone's idea is to make it seem so familiar but so different at the same time. He turns up the music and listens to it. I love a good Beatles cover song, they are all like little puzzles you have to listen to really closely to find out which song it is. But I never figure them out 'til the end . . . the last piece of a problem is always the hardest to find, but I've got a plan.

SCENE NINE

Joel: What time did you say it was?

Turrin: I didn't.

Lucy: Joel, none of us have watches.

Joel: Right, sorry.

Silence.

Joel: Lucy, does everyone always sing you "Lucy In The Sky With Diamonds"?

Lucy: Sometimes.

Joel: Does it annoy you?

Lucy: Not really. I liked that song a lot, when I was little—

Turrin cuts her off.

Turrin: Wasn't that song about LSD?

Lucy: No, I think someone made that up.

Turrin: I don't like The Beatles.

Lucy: How can you not like The Beatles?

Turrin: I just don't.

Lucy: So, who do you like?

Turrin: The Beach Boys.

Lucy: . . . Oh.

Joel: The Beach Boys had some good ones, but they didn't have John Lennon. He wrote some good songs. "Hey Jude" is my favourite.

Turrin: Paul McCartney wrote "Hey Jude".

Joel: No he didn't. John Lennon wrote it for Julian Lennon, for his birthday or something.

Turrin: Paul McCartney wrote "Hey Jude" for Julian Lennon when his parents got divorced.

Lucy: For someone who doesn't like The Beatles, you sure know a lot about them.

Turrin: Who doesn't?

Joel: All I know is that they wrote most of their songs on or about drugs.

Lucy: Not all their songs, maybe two or three.

Joel pulls out a deck of cards from his jacket.

Joel: Wanna play?

Lucy: Why didn't you bring those out before?

Joel: I forgot I had them.

SCENE TEN

The elevator version of "Paperback Writer" plays in the background. Casey is watching old footage of The Beatles.

Casey: Thank you for having me . . . Thank you for having me . . . on your show . . . on YOUR show . . . Hello public, no . . . Hello viewers and thanks for having me here.

He continues mouthing thanks and practicing his words.

The lights come up. Lucy is pacing now. She looks worried.

Lucy: We need to get out of here. I have a weird feeling about this. Why haven't they come to get us? What's taking him so long? Where is that guy? Help!

Joel: You're not shouting loud enough.

Lucy: Help me then. On three. One, two, Help! . . . Why didn't you yell?

Joel: You said on three, which means one, two, three, help, not one, two, help.

Lucy: Fine, on three. One, two, three. *She and Joel yell together.* HELP!

Joel: Help!

Lucy: I doubt they can hear us. *Starts to push all the buttons.* Maybe one of these buttons will trigger it to move . . . I need to get out of here.

Turrin: Lucy, stop that, we don't know if this thing is stable.

Lucy: Hey wait, I think we're moving . . . look it's moving up.

Turrin: Lucy! *To Joel.* This is not supposed to move.

Lucy: Who cares? It's moving. We can get off on a higher floor.

Joel: Turrin, do you have the time?

Turrin: Fuck off, Joel.

Lucy: Don't worry Joel, I'm going to have us out of here in a minute. . . . Wait, I think we stopped.

Casey: Hello?

Lucy: Hello? Casey? Look, this is ridiculous. There is no way that it takes you this long to find your tools. You need to get up here . . . We are now on the twenty-sixth floor . . . If we are not out of here in five min—

Casey: Why did you do that? It's going to be very hard now, the signal is fading and I can't see the picture.

Lucy: Pardon?

Joel: Could you stop talking and get us out?

Lucy: What does he mean he can't see the picture?

Turrin: There's a security camera over there.

All three look closely into the camera.

Joel: He can see us? Then why isn't he doing anything?

Casey: You shouldn't have done that.

Turrin: All right, just come and get us.

Silence.

Joel: So, where were we with the card game?

Lucy: I'm not playing cards again.

Silence.

Turrin puts his hand in his pocket and finds a bag of candy.

Turrin: Hey look what I found? Want some?

Lucy: No thank you.

Turrin: Are you sure, they're really good.

Lucy: Okay. *She puts it in her mouth.* Yeah, it's good.

Turrin: If you bite into the middle it has that fizzy stuff inside.

Lucy: It's not fizzing.

Turrin: Really? Weird?

Silence.

Joel: Hey Lucy, wanna play Rock, Paper, Scissors?

Lucy: Not really.

Joel: Come on, I'm bored.

Lucy: Okay.

They start to play.

Cut to TV3. An interviewer talks to two guys on the street.

Interviewer: Why do you think people like Turrin so much?

Guy One: 'Cause he's awesome, and he doesn't take shit.

Another guy runs into the shot, his hand is outstretched and full of candy.

Guy Two: Hey! Look what I found, want some? They're fizzy inside. . . .

Both guys start laughing and then start to chant, "Turrin, Turrin!"

SCENE TWELVE

The original version of "Sgt. Pepper's Lonely Hearts Club Band" plays over this monologue.

Casey: Barbara Walters, thank you so much for inviting me here. I'm honoured. First, can I start by saying, it's wonderful to be here. It's certainly a thrill. You're such a lovely audience. *He pretends that people are clapping.* Stop, really. I didn't expect this much fanfare. I'm just a regular guy like everyone else. I'm just honoured that everyone has connected with my work. But, really, I'm the same old guy I've always been. Luckily, I have a very supportive family. They always keep me grounded. I have to take out the garbage like everyone else. Ha, Ha, Ha. Anyway, should we show the clip of my newest film? Yes, it's more of a dramatic piece. It stars John Ritter and I also have a small cameo in the film. So here it is. Sit back and let the evening go. I hope you enjoy the show.

SCENE THIRTEEN

They are still playing Rock, Paper, Scissors. Lucy is visibly tired and can hardly concentrate.

Joel: Come on Lucy, pay attention.

Lucy: I can't play any more. I'm sorry, I'm really tired.

Turrin: What's wrong?

Lucy: I don't know, I can hardly keep my eyes open.

Turrin: Maybe you're sick.

Lucy is leaning on Joel. He puts his arm around her.

Joel: *To Turrin.* What time is it?

Turrin: Time.

We hear the crescendo to "A Day in the Life." It starts to build.

Turrin: Hey Lucy, can I ask you a question? Can I kiss you? . . . One kiss between friends?

Lucy looks up at Joel. She is visibly tired.

Turrin: Joel doesn't mind, come on.

Lucy slowly starts to pass out and Joel stands up and lets her fall to the floor. She is facing the audience. He turns his back to her, The lights start to dim. Lucy starts slowly repeating, "Stop watching, turn it off."

Turrin: Joel. It's time. . . . Are you ready? Lucy, look at me. . . . Look at me! Good, her pupils are dilated.

Joel: *Whispering.* You shouldn't take candy from strangers. Okay let's do this.

Turrin: She's not out yet.

Joel: She's supposed to be out by now. I don't want to hear this.

Lucy: Stop WATCHING. Turn It Off!!!

Blackout.

SCENE FOURTEEN

Casey stands in horror in front of the screen on his desk. This scene is timed perfectly with the last sound of the crescendo of "A Day in the Life", the piano silences. He turns quickly to the audience and, in a panic, grabs his tool belt. He goes to run off but stops and grabs a VHS tape sitting on his desk and sticks it in his back pocket. This must be clear to the audience. As he runs off, TV 2 starts to play as if it was a window into Casey's head. As this starts we hear the "Woke up got out of bed . . ." part of "A Day in the Life".

Frame One: A camera turns on and we see Casey for a split second.

Frame Two: We see Casey's feet as he walks down the hall into the bathroom.

Frame Three: The camera is put on the sink and we see upside down footage of Casey brushing his teeth.

Frame Four: We see a hand putting toast in the toaster.

Frame Five: A hand grabs a jacket.

Frame Six: We see feet again, this time they are walking down the street.

Frame Seven: A shot of a street from a rooftop, a leaf blows onto the lens, the camera is readjusted, we see Casey's face for a moment.

Frame Eight: On the same street we see Lucy walking with a lot of stuff, she drops her papers and has to pick them up. Extreme close-up on Lucy.

Frame Nine: We watch a bunch of people in an elevator.

Frame Ten: We see another group in an elevator, this time with Joel, close-up on Joel's face and the tape is paused.

Frame Eleven: Another elevator group, this time with Turrin, we see a close up and then the tape is paused.

As the song cuts to the second crescendo, we see the three in an elevator. We see them shot at every angle as if there were cameras everywhere inside the elevator. We see Lucy's legs, arms, etc. The shots should look as if Joel and Turrin had hidden cameras on them. The shots should recreate some of the events that have already happened in the elevator, but at a different and obscured angle. The last shot is Lucy's face.

SCENE FIFTEEN

The scene starts as if Casey has just opened the door to the elevator; all his tools are on the floor. Lucy is in a heap on the floor. You can't see her face.

Joel: *Eating a sandwich.* That took a long time, Casey. What did we tell you? No longer than three hours. What were you thinking?

Casey: What did you guys do? What did you do?

Turrin: What does it look like to you?

Casey: You guys said you'd be funny. This was supposed to be fun. I'm the director. . . . I'm the director.

Joel: Whatever, Casey. All we agreed to is that we would do the parts you asked. You didn't specify what else could happen.

Casey: I think you hurt her. She's not gonna come back for the second episode.

Turrin: Casey, listen to me, there is no TV show and you're not a director. Okay? This is not a TV show we're making here.

Casey: No! This is a TV show. It's my TV show.

Joel: Face the facts. You're a fuckin' idiot, Casey. No one in their right mind would give you a TV show.

Casey: *We see a glimpse of a different Casey.* What did you say? What did you say? *He goes after Joel and grabs him by the throat.* I'm not an idiot! Did you hear me? *Turrin pulls him off.*

Turrin: What the hell are you doing? Calm down!.

Casey: Sorry guys. Sorry, I didn't mean it.

Joel: That's better, and what the hell were you thinking, yelling in my ear about that jacket shit. I told you I would, so I did. *Pulls out the earphone out of his ear.* You almost blew it for us.

Casey: I'm sorry. I wasn't thinking.

Turrin: No, you weren't.

Joel: *Goes into his bag takes out a script.* Look right here on page seven. "Slowly talk about the heat, then proceed with Three's Company Jacket scene." The key word there is slowly, Casey. I don't appreciate you yelling at me when I'm following your stupid script.

Casey: You're right, Joel. Sorry.

Turrin: So hand over the tape. We have to go.

Casey: I didn't tape anything. It was a rehearsal.

Joel: *Starts to search him.* What's this then? What is this Casey!?! You trying to keep it from us?

Casey: No, I'm sorry.

Turrin: That would have been a really bad idea keeping our tape. You don't want more bad things to happen? Do You?

Casey: No . . . Lucy are you awake?

Joel: Don't touch her, she'll be fine.

Casey: You're not supposed to hurt girls.

Turrin: All right, all right we have to go.

Casey: What about my picture? You promised I'd get the picture.

Turrin: What, this? *He pulls out a picture of John Ritter.* Is this what you wanted, Casey?

Casey: Guys, give it.

Turrin: I don't know? You left us in there a pretty long time.

Casey: Sorry, Sorry. . . . Guys, I just want the picture.

Joel: I don't think we can forgive that, Casey. Plus, you didn't really hold up your end of the deal.

Casey: Neither did you.

Turrin starts to crumple up the paper in front of Casey.

Casey: No, don't do that. No . . . Please. *He cries holding on to the piece of paper.*

Joel: Hey Lucy, Lucy. *He turns to Turrin.* Good, she's still out. *He and Turrin exit.*

Turrin: *As he exits.* See ya around Casey.

They exit, leaving both Casey and Lucy on the floor. After they exit, Casey looks up as "Lucy In The Sky With Diamonds" plays. He goes over to Lucy to check if she's alive. He takes all her things and puts them into her purse. He takes a cellphone out of his pocket and dials.

Casey: *Starts crying.* Hello 911 emergency? I just found this lady in my building . . . There's been a rape. *As he talks he walks over to his desk the stage lights come up on that side of the stage. He walks over to the surveillance tape and starts rewinding it, so that the audience realizes that he still has the actual surveillance tape.* I think she's hurt very badly . . . My name is Casey Ginter . . . Yes on twenty-third street . . . the elevator. *He finds the beginning and stops the tape. In a very un-Casey-like voice,* Thank you.

He immediately stops crying. "Lucy in the Sky with Diamonds" starts to play again. He looks to the audience and smiles.

SCENE TEN

A news broadcaster sits at a desk with Casey who now looks like a bad John Lennon impersonator. This interview can also be done as an audio clip, with the audience sitting in darkness.

Broadcaster: The infamous "rape tape" will go on sale today at midnight. The fever for this real life drama has caught everyone by surprise. Pirated copies of the tape have already been selling for up to two hundred dollars for a preview of the three hour long drama that has been nick-named *Code Word: Time* after the secret word devised by the two assailants as to when the attack would occur. Shirts of the three stars of the tape as well as hats and key chains have been selling out in stores across the country. The success of this tape has lead to the new reality series by creator Casey Ginter. He joins us in the studio today. Hello, Casey.

Casey: Hello, Graham. Thank you for having me.

Graham: So Casey, how have you been dealing with your new-found fame?

Casey: Well, I still have to take out the garbage like everyone else. *He laughs.* But seriously, I'm just honoured to have the opportunity to create a new type of television. The fact that the response has been overwhelming is just an added bonus.

Graham: Casey, what is your reaction toward the controversy around *Code Word: Time*? Critics say that it has been the catalyst for a new low in television programming.

Casey: Well, everything that becomes successful always gets criticized at the beginning, but the new episodes are quite different. . . .

Graham: What is your response to the movement to have your show cancelled out of respect for Lucy Williams?

Casey: . . . The show is quite different now. *Code Word: Time* was just the first episode. I didn't have any control over the events that took place. My lawyer already released a statement about this. . . .

Graham: Can you tell us how the tape got released?

Casey: Like I've said before, I gave the tapes over to the authorities. It must have leaked from within. I had nothing to do with it.

Graham: Do you feel you owe Ms. Williams an apology?

Close up on Casey as he sweats. . . . Fade out. There is a pause. The audience sits in darkness and then we see the following words scroll across the screen. They can be accompanied by a voice over.

Tonight we bring you the television première of one of the most controversial reality programs to come along in years. Please note some scenes are graphic and may not be suitable for all. Viewer discretion is advised. And now, *Code Word: Time.*

As the string version of "Eleanor Rigby" plays, the tape plays and we see the three standing in the elevator like they were at the beginning of the show. Credits start to roll down the screen. The actors come out for a curtain call and stand directly in front of the TV. House lights go up. The tape is still playing. . . .

END

Mathew Kloster and Matt Alden in *Beneath the Deep Blue Sky*.

Beneath the Deep Blue Sky

Rob Bartel

When *Beneath The Deep Blue Sky* first came into my hands, the support material was almost as thick as the script itself. The story of the script's genesis extended back to a conversation that had occurred in a line-up outside of a venue at the Edmonton Fringe in 2000. The package also came with the biographies and career goals of the proposed artistic team. Usually Nextfest will put the production teams together, but this was a package deal that included a script, a director, a stage manager, and a designer.

The aforementioned conversation between Rob Bartel, Rachel Rudd, and Beth Mackey was about the type of company they wanted to form ("BRR in the Wings") and the type of theatre they wanted to create. Rob Bartel had a vision of what he wanted to write but did not have the key to unlock it. After they saw the show they had been waiting to see, he turned to his collaborators and told him he knew his path. The show was *Love Letters From The Unabomber* by Jeff Page and Wes Borg (performed by Jeff Page). So Nextfest made the counter-proposal to BRR that if they wanted to work together, then Nextfest's terms were that they would have to work with Jeff Page serving as a production advisor to the production team. They were more than elated.

We also insisted that they utilize a multimedia design and that Nextfest could find that designer for them. (Once again, they were elated and slightly confused as to why Nextfest's terms of acceptance were less like hoops to jump through and more like gifts to play with.) Local photographer Ian Jackson was more than established as a photojournalist but had just begun to play with digital projection technology and was itching for an opportunity to practice it.

The play is obsessed with technology and our relationship to technology. These elements can conspire to some fascinating spectacle if you have the tools and know how to use them. The movement of ideas and images in the play is captivating, and if one has the ability to visually present the experience of the computer when presenting this play, you should. However, then the question of what the play is not raises its head, and herein is the difficulty in staging it. It is not a play about war or greed or lust or revenge or any of the other primal urges that we are compelled to watch acted out in the darkened rooms we call theatres. The play contains thematically unified ideas and images, which perhaps motivate the movement of the play more than its plot and characters do. The flow of ideas is guided more by Boolean operators (search engine grammar) than by natural human dialogue; *Beneath The Deep Blue Sky* is a hyper-link play.

As the play teaches us, it's very easy to get distracted by technology at the expense of human contact. One shouldn't fall into this trap when presenting the play. That's why I think the most important component to any director's vision of this play should be the idea of connections: connecting to the Internet, connecting random ideas to one another, but most importantly connecting to Daniel. While I find all the characters presented by Daniel to be fascinating, ultimately those characters do not have the ability to reach out and physically connect or be connected to Peter. The only person who can do that is the homeless man Daniel himself. I think you have to make him the most important persona in the play, otherwise you might find yourself forgetting about him.

At NeXtFest 2002, *Beneath The Deep Blue Sky* had two visual design components. The stage was divided left and right into areas with an Internet café and Peter's bedroom (complete with a live goldfish that lived in my office between shows . . . he/she died shortly after the end of the Festival). The set also incorporated Tetris shaped blocks manipulated by the actors to shape other acting areas. The projection design was primarily used to reflect the mind of the computer, yet was present quite consistently throughout the play.

– S.P.

An early draft of *Beneath the Deep Blue Sky* was workshopped and produced at the Carnival of Shrieking Youth, May 2001, in Edmonton. It was directed by Andrew Thompson and won First Prize, going on to help launch the Carnival's first season in Calgary later that summer. The play prèmiered at NeXtFest 2002 at the Roxy Theatre with the following team:

Peter: *Matt Alden*
Daniel: *Matthew Kloster*
God / Deep Blue: *Stanley Woo*
Director: *Beth Mackey*
Stage Manager: *Rachel Rudd*
Stage Design: *James Bylund*
Projection Design: *Ian Jackson*
Lil' Helper: *Jeff Page*

The BRR in the Wings theatre collective went on to remount *Beneath the Deep Blue Sky* at the Edmonton International Fringe Festival in August 2002, with the same cast. A new book version of the play was published in October 2004 by New Bard Press, a theatre micropress of which Rob is a founding member.

CHARACTERS

God: Ageless. Creator of existence. Offstage voice.

Peter: 25 years old. A disheveled, over-stimulated Internet addict and technophile, starved of meaningful human contact, plagued by tech related visions and hallucinations presumably related to undiagnosed schizophrenic tendencies.

Daniel: 19 years old. A young panhandler who is far from home and is beginning to grow used to the transient life. Daniel takes on the various roles of Peter's visions based on historical figures as follows:

Alexey Pajitnov: The Soviet computer programmer who created Tetris.

Garry Kasparov: The Russian chess grandmaster. Suffered a highly publicized loss against an IBM supercomputer named Deep Blue.

Mathias Rust: A teenager who flew a small plane from West Germany into Moscow's Red Square in 1987.

Prof. David Cope: The American creator of 'Emmy,' a computer program capable of composing original music often indistinguishable from the best of the classical canon.

Mr. Fish: A brightly colored fish kept in a small bowl in Peter's bachelor suite. Non-speaking role.

Deep Blue: Chess-playing IBM supercomputer. Webmaster of the Celestial Domain. Benevolent angelic functionary for the digital age. Offstage voice.

A video projector presents the following two character as unspoken text.

Eliza / Dr. Joseph Weizenbaum: Eliza is a simplistic artificial intelligence program with the personality of a Rogerian psychotherapist designed in the 1960s by computer scientist Joseph Weizenbaum.

THE SETTING

The text of the play makes reference to an apartment above Edmonton's Whyte Avenue; however, producers are encouraged to think of the play as set in the city in which it is being produced. On opposite sides of the stage are Peter's unkempt bachelor's suite and a nearby Internet Café, both buried in a commercial district of a Canadian city. Between the two is a neutral exterior space where Daniel panhandles for change. Winter is approaching. Each scene represents a new month, beginning with September.

Peter (Matt Alden) struggles to connect to the
Internet in *Beneath the Deep Blue Sky.*
PHOTOGRAPH COURTESY OF DAVID WILLIAMSON

Beneath the Deep Blue Sky

*Peter is in his claustrophobic, above-shop apartment along
Edmonton's Whyte Avenue. A goldfish swims in a bowl beside
his bed and a laptop computer rests open beside him. It is night,
nearing dawn. Outside the nearby Internet Café, Daniel is
curled up and sleeping soundly, a chess set in play beside him.
From offstage, we hear the voice of God. Peter ignores him, his
attention riveted on making fish faces at the bowl.*

God: *Offstage.* Peter . . . . Peter . . . . Peter . . .

Peter: *To Mr. Fish.* I'm becoming just like you, aren't I . . .
Trapped in this tiny place, never sleeping, never blink-
ing . . .

God: *Offstage.* Peter . . .

Peter: *To Mr. Fish.* Not that it matters. Asleep, awake, I get all
the dreams I need, regardless, my fingers twitching, spastic,
clicking . . . You can't see me, can you. You press up against
the glass and all you see are reflections of yourself.

God: *Offstage.* Peter, it's time . . .

Peter: *To Mr. Fish.* Yeah, tell me about it. You can still hear me,
though. I can tell, Mr. Fish, oh I can tell . . . You twitch
every time you hear my voice, don't you. You turn around,
searching for me, but all you ever find are visions of yourself, more fish all distorted by the glass. . . . Yeah, well, I
gotta go to work.

*Peter turns to the laptop and presses Ctrl-Alt-Delete. It does
nothing so he tries again. Frustrated, he pounds random keys,
then snaps the laptop shut.*

Peter: *To Mr. Fish.* Yeah, well you know what? I can still see a
game of Tetris I played five years ago. Oh yeah. Move by
move, block by falling block. Other times it's bar upon bar
of written music, streaming past with all the chaos of blackbirds in the wind. Sometimes, it's a thousand paintings of
people posed within a lush and vibrant junglescape. On-
line, off-line? It doesn't make a difference anymore because

there in the midst of it, guess what I hear, Mr. Fish . . . No, no, that's crazy—I hear the accusing voice of God.

God: *Offstage.* Peter, the world is ending . . . slowly . . .

Peter: *To Mr. Fish.* See? *To God.* What do you want from me?

God: *Offstage.* I . . . I wanted you to hear me say I'm sorry . . . I didn't mean for it to be like this. . . .

Peter: *To Mr. Fish.* Yeah, if only you could see me, Mr. Fish. I've been on-line for three days straight but my modem's trashed from overheating. . . . Hey, any idea when the sun's going to come up? The—The Internet café down the street opens up at eight—Look, I won't be long, okay? . . . Don't go anywhere.

Peter starts putting on his jacket to brave the cold.

Peter: Yeah, here I am, face pressed against the glass, my thoughts all reflecting each other to infinity, looping back on themselves like a chess game, playing and replaying itself before me in a million permutations. . . .

Peter approaches Daniel, who is now playing a game of chess against himself.

Peter: Café open?

Daniel: No one by yet.

Peter: Oh.

Daniel: Spare some change?

Peter: Yeah, right, you take debit?

Daniel: Debit?

Peter: Nothing, never mind. Junkie's joke.

Daniel: Jus' enough for a coffee at the bus station, hey?

Peter: Look, some of us have bigger problems than missing out on a cup of coffee, all right?

Daniel: Was jus' a coffee, asshole . . .

Daniel transforms into a vision of Alexey Pajitnov, the creator of Tetris.

Daniel: *As Alexey Pajitnov.* I took my lunch—

Peter: *Trying to tune Alexey Pajitnov out.* And there it comes, one of the visions: A little snippet of my life, strung together with electrical tape, and buried cable, and the knowledge that behind that window, through that door, there's a computer and it's connected and I can be okay for only two dollars every ten minutes.

Danel: *As Alexey Pajitnov.* I took my lunch one day in Mayakovsky Square, in the gardens there—

Peter: Ten minutes here, ten minutes there, a thousand little puzzle pieces falling, one by one, to take their place in my life—

Daniel: *As Alexey Pajitnov.* —and as I dusted the crumbs into the pond, I looked in and saw the bright fish trying to hide themselves amidst the dull grey rocks and sand—

Peter: —and if you can complete a line, poof, it disappears and you win points, glorious points, but those puzzle pieces just keep falling faster and faster, piling up with all their gaps and holes—

Daniel: *As Alexey Pajitnov.* —and I said "That is how we people of Russia are. We want to be invisible, we all want so badly to fit in." When I invented Tetris later on that year, it was that thought I had in mind. . . .

Peter: *To Alexey Pajitnov.* Invented Tetris? I was addicted to that game as a kid. It was so . . . efficient. The art in the background was always changing, always new, always forbidden.

Daniel: *As Alexey Patijnov.* Yes, the art! I filled it with pictures from our "official" history, you know: St. Basil's Cathedral at the beginning, Sputnik's launch at the end. But in the middle I hid a message: a picture of that young West German boy, Mathias Rust, landing his tiny plane in Red Square in broad daylight. I wanted to tell the West that we are not dead here yet and that the space between us is not uncrossable. . . .

Silence. Daniel becomes himself again. He returns to his chess set and makes a move.

Daniel: Hey, man, you all right?

Peter: No. You?

Daniel: Cold.

Peter: The day'll warm up.

Daniel: . . .Café opened mebbe five minutes ago . . . Didn't wanna disturb you, but you wanted in.

Peter: . . .Thanks . . .

Peter enters the café, takes off his jacket.

Peter: I fold myself into my usual seat with my usual cup of coffee that will sit there, beside me, slowly growing cold.

The lines of Dr. Joseph Weizenbaum, Peter's psychologist, are projected against an upstage screen.

Weizen: Hello, Peter.

Peter: Hello, Dr. Weizenbaum.

Weizen: How shall we begin?

Peter: I saw another vision today.

Weizen: Do you believe it's normal that you saw another vision today?

Peter: Define normal . . .

Weizen: I see . . .

Peter: All of their faces are starting to blend together. I saw a panhandler this morning and I think he's real but he looked just like another vision. Only half-real, somehow.

Weizen: What resemblance do you see?

Peter: I . . . I don't know.

Weizen: Why do you not know?

Peter: . . .Last night, God told me that the world is ending.

Weizen: I see . . .

Peter: It left me thinking that—

Weizen: Please go on.

Peter: Well, it left me thinking what is the point of it all? Why are we here, you know?

Weizen: Does that question interest you?

Peter: I don't know what interests me anymore. . . .

Silence. Dr. Weizenbaum fades.

Peter: Once you're familiar enough with the Internet, it's like one of those inkblot tests psychologists use to trick you into telling them about yourself? There's more random information out there than we could ever wrap our heads around, so the uncanny machine asks us to make up keywords, right? And it digs, digs deep to find them wherever they may lie . . . And what it finds is like a drug.

I found this site called MetaSpy . . . Ever wonder what the rest of the world is searching for? It's all there, a random selection of terms that other people have submitted, automatically refreshed and reselected every fifteen seconds.

From offstage, we hear the voice of Deep Blue, Webmaster of the Celestial Domain. Daniel re-emerges, lovingly unfolds his chess set, and begins to set up another game against himself.

Blue: *Offstage.* Footstool: Ottoman—

Peter: Denmark financial statistics—

Blue: *Offstage.* Foreign relations: Ivory Coast—

Peter: Anger management—

Blue: *Offstage.* Beth Dubray St. Peters—

Peter: Ohio golf courses —

Blue: *Offstage.* Color Yellow—

Peter: Mpeg layer 3—

Blue: *Offstage.* Shoelaces—

Peter: Circe, Greek goddess—

Blue: *Offstage.* Corkboard—

Peter: Renovation + windows—

Blue: *Offstage.* San Francisco earthquake—

Peter: Duke + sweatshops—

Blue: *Offstage.* Vegan recipes—

Peter: News, May 12—

Blue: *Offstage.* Negotiation abstracts—

Peter: "Why I Need an Education"—

Blue: *Offstage.* JFK Conspiracy—

Peter: Rococo style—

Blue: *Offstage.* Zodo, inc.—

Peter: Motel 6 —

Blue: *Offstage.* Lapis lazuli—

Peter: Life simulator—

Blue: *Offstage.* Muppets: Japanese—

Peter: Cheese cartoon commercial—

Blue: *Offstage.* Thermostat repair—

Peter: Yogic levitation—

Blue: *Offstage.* Hiking boots—

Peter: Parker cartridge bilge pumps —

Blue: *Offstage.* Electrostatic hum —

Peter: Confession of Faith—

Blue: *Offstage.* Apartment rentals for creatives—

Peter: Ancient Egyptian cosmetics—

Blue: *Offstage.* Job interview tips —

Peter: Entry-level Internet technology jobs —

Blue: *Offstage.* Spirit of fear —

Peter: Boxproject—circumcision—Utah Grieving Counsel—
Preteen Lolita pics—Las Vegas weather—Blind Date
TV—Maps—Oregon nudist clubs—Ludismo . . . Free Butt
Thong Galleries!!!

Silence.

Peter: So, uh, of course I click it. And I click again and once more and—aw damn! —before I know it, I'm at another site, something about chess, I gather, but it's hard to tell because everything's written in Russian. There's a mirror site in English, though, so I click again.

Daniel: *As Garry Kasparov, a World Chess Champion ultimately defeated by Deep Blue.* What do you want? Can't you see the clock is ticking?

Peter: Sorry, I was looking for . . . something else.

Daniel: *As Garry Kasparov.* There is nothing else! There is only this game!

Peter: I said I'm sorry!

Daniel: *As Garry Kasparov.* No, you've come to see me play, haven't you? Come to see me pace back and forth like a caged animal? Come to see a computer wipe its ass with Garry Kasparov? Well I will beat this . . . thing!

Peter: Kasparov?

Daniel: *As Garry Kasparov.* Go away! The clock is ticking! . . . Do you even understand what I'm doing here? This chess match is a defence of the whole human race.

Peter: Russian Grandmaster, once considered the best chess player in history . . .

Daniel: *As Garry Kasparov.* Ever get the feeling that the computer is trying to trick you, that it is ENJOYING its position on the board? That it's laughing at you? It never tires, never makes a tactical mistake, never gives you a break.

Peter: . . . defeated at his own game by a machine, an IBM supercomputer capable of calculating two million possible moves a second . . . They called it Deep Blue.

God: *Offstage.* Garry . . .

Daniel: *As Garry Kasparov.* Quiet!

God: *Offstage.* Garry, it's time . . .

Daniel: *As Garry Kasparov.* It's over! I quit, all right!? Are you happy? Do you even understand? We're dead here . . .

Peter: Is it all inevitable, Kasparov?

Daniel: *As Garry Kasparov, to Peter.* It played like God.

God: *Offstage.* . . . It played like Kasparov. . . .

Silence.

Peter: *To God.* The end of the world is coming, isn't it?

God: *Offstage.* Yes it is. Slowly . . .

Peter: Slowly . . . God?

God: *Offstage.* Yes, Peter?

Peter: I want to be able to sleep tonight.

God: *Offstage.* All right.

Peter: I want to sleep for an entire month.

God: *Offstage.* All right . . . And Peter?

Peter: Yeah?

God: *Offstage.* Don't forget your coffee.

Peter: Why? I don't want it.

God: *Offstage.* The panhandler outside—his name is Daniel. . . .

Peter puts on his jacket and picks up the coffee cup.

Peter: And there you have it: Little snippets of my life, strung together with visions and buried cable and the knowledge that someday this will all be over, whether we want it to be or not.

Peter exits the Internet Café.

Daniel: Spare some change?

Peter: How about some coffee?

Daniel: Yeah?

Peter: It—It's a bit cold. . . .

Daniel: Thanks.

Peter: Didn't come with a lid.

Daniel: 'At's okay.

Peter: . . . Is—Is your name Daniel?

Daniel: Yeah.

Peter: . . . Take care, Daniel.

Daniel: All right . . . Hey, you play chess?

Peter: Yeah.

Daniel: Maybe we should play sometime.

Peter: Yeah . . .

Peter moves on, toward his apartment.

Peter: If I look up, I'll see a star or two piercing the streetlights' glow. But that would mean admitting that it's night already and that I've somehow missed the light of this September day. As I enclose myself within this glassy bowl, I can hear traffic passing in the distance and the hum of the telephone wires. I lower myself to bed and sleep.

SCENE TWO: OCTOBER

Peter's claustrophobic apartment. Peter sleeps fitfully, caught in a nightmare of a West German youth, Mathias Rust.

Daniel: *As Mathias Rust.* My name is Mathias Rust. When I was nineteen, I rented a bone-white Cessna, intending to fly into Soviet airspace until I was shot down by the red-starred MiGs . . . I expected all the wrath of God and Lenin but where I begged for the missile's thunder, all I found was silence. Where all I wanted were angry clouds of chaff and spray, you taunted me with a deep, blue, Russian sky. . . .

Well damn you both, then! Damn you to hell and capitalism!! I meant to die that day but you know the only corpse I got to see? Moscow's; pale and bloated, rising up along the far horizon! . . . I wanted to be a martyr—I wanted it to end that way. Instead, beneath your empty sky, I took that Cessna down low over the domes of St. Basil's Cathedral and landed it there in Red Square's heart. I surrendered, I gave up—a fucking prophet, not a martyr.

"Better dead than red," they say. Yeah, well some of us don't get that choice. We're not dead here yet. There aren't any spaces between us that can't be crossed. . . .

Peter wakes from the nightmare. Silence as he catches his breath.

Peter: It's October, isn't it? It's October and it's . . . finally gone and silent, like the sound of water flowing. Silent, like a gust of wind. Silent. Like God Himself was holding His breath to give me room to speak. *To God* God?

Silence.

Peter: God!?

Daniel curls up beside the café door. From offstage, we once again hear the voice of the Webmaster, Deep Blue.

Blue: *Offstage.* Error 404 [File Not Found]: This god is no longer available—The god you were looking for might have been removed, moved, had its name changed, or is temporarily unavailable.

Peter: *To Deep Blue.* Had its . . . name changed?

Blue: *Offstage.* We are sorry for any inconvenience this may have caused.

Peter: What have you done with Him?!

Blue: *Offstage.* If you are experiencing difficulties viewing this page, please e-mail the Webmaster of the Celestial Domain: DeepBlue@Heaven.org.

Peter puts on his jacket.

Peter: *To Mr. Fish.* Sorry, Mr. Fish. I gotta go.

Peter flees to the café where Daniel is setting up the chess set for another game.

Daniel: Spare some change?

Peter: Is the café open?

Daniel: Nobody's come by all day.

Peter: Oh.

Silence.

Daniel: Sure you can't spare some change?

Silence.

Daniel: I'll take debit.

Peter: Doesn't matter, the lines are down or a router's blown somewhere. My connection's not working at home, either.

Daniel: MasterCard?

Peter: They all use the same system.

Daniel: Cash? I've got change for a nickel.

Peter: Haven't used cash in years. Sorry . . .

Daniel: Canadian Tire money?

Silence.

Peter: . . . Are you cold, Daniel?

Daniel: A little.

Peter: Here, I'll trade you jackets.

Daniel: All right . . . What's your name, anyway?

Peter: Me? Peter . . . Here, take it.

They trade jackets and settle in against the cold.

Daniel: You still want a game . . . ?

Peter: Yeah, I guess . . . Not much choice, is there?

They absorb themselves in the chess game.

Peter: . . . Any snow come yet this year?

Daniel: A coupla times at night. Always gone by morning, though. Mostly we get frost. Ice in the puddles by the car wash.

Peter: . . . It's pretty how it turns all the leaves yellow.

Daniel: See that one? It's a mountain ash—the first to lose its leaves each year.

Peter: It looks dead.

Daniel: No . . . It's just waiting.

Peter: What for?

Daniel: For the birds to come. They eat its berries. Pick it clean.

Silence.

Peter: So is this what you do all day, Daniel?

Daniel: What?

Peter: Sit around and play chess against yourself.

Daniel: I dunno. I bum money. When I get enough, I go down to the bus station and get a coffee. One of the guys there sometimes packs an extra sandwich in his lunch for me.

Peter: And when he's not working or when no one gives you money?

Daniel: I sit around, watch people. Play 'gainst myself, wait for the birds. You?

Peter: Play against yourself, huh?

Daniel: Serious, what do you do all day?

Peter: I don't know. I talk to people. Sometimes I talk to this guy named Cope, he's a music professor at UCLA and he wrote this computer program named Emmy that composes its own music. You feed it some Chopin or Beethoven and it—and it spits out new stuff in that same style . . .

Daniel: *As Professor David Cope,* Emmy's creator. What can I say about Emmy? She's just there—bar upon bar, a million notes, all the fury of blackbirds in the wind.

Peter: Cope presented a paper of Emmy's compositions and a distinguished German music critic leapt onstage during one of his lectures and punched him in the face. At the top of his voice, he kept yelling "Musik ist tot!" Music is destroyed . . .

Daniel: *As Professor David Cope.* Emmy has no model whatsoever of life experiences. She has no sense of herself, has no sense of Chopin, has never heard a note of music, has no trace in her of where we have always thought music comes from. Not a trace. A friend asked me: "Is a composer's soul irrelevant to the music?" To him, Emmy seemed such an absolute tragedy because, throughout his entire life, he'd been moved by music. He'd always felt that it brought him into contact with the absolute essence of humanity.

Peter: *To Daniel.* Musik ist tot . . . Then there's this abstractionist painter. He built a robot named Aaron that creates thousands of paintings of its own devising. Aaron uses actual paintbrushes to paint them and he—IT rinses with care every time IT switches colours. . . .

Daniel makes a move on the chessboard, putting Peter in check.

Daniel: You don't talk to no one like that.

Peter: Sure I—Sure I do, in my own way.

Daniel: Why are you tellin' me all this, anyways?

Peter: I don't know, Daniel, I just—I think it's important, somehow . . . Sometimes I get frightened by these things but, every now and then, I can hold all the pieces in my head at once just for a moment and . . . and I realize that it's so beautiful.

Silence.

Peter: *To audience.* . . . And all the while as I slept, I dreamt I was a child, flying towards some infinite horizon, lost and low on fuel beneath that deep blue sky. . . .

Daniel: *As Mathias Rust.* When I was nineteen, I pierced the Iron Curtain and saw what was beyond.

Peter: When I was nineteen, I was drifting aimlessly through university.

Daniel: *As Mathias Rust.* For my crimes, they dismantled my plane and locked me in a Russian jail . . . When I returned home to West Germany, eighteen months later, they were selling t-shirts with my name.

Peter: I . . . I just dabbled in History and—and Commerce. . . .

Daniel: *As Mathias Rust.* I got work at a hospital in Rissen and I fell in love with Anja, who worked there as a nurse. When she said it was over, I stabbed her with a knife. For my crimes, they threw me back in jail.

Peter: I had no passions! No purpose . . .

Daniel: *As Mathias Rust.* When all my terms were served, I went back to Russia where I hid myself from God and Lenin and tried to fit in like a bright fish amongst all the dull grey rocks and sand.

Peter: But you know what? Piece by falling piece, it all started coming down and building up and all I ever learned was just how necessary it must be to be happy! . . . My life had become a Tetris game.

Daniel: *As Alexey Pajitnov.* Do not think about it too much.

Peter: *To Alexey Pajitnov.* No?

Daniel: *As Alexey Pajitnov.* No. You must FEEL the puzzle. You are a bright fish trying to hide from the man who feeds you crumbs in Mayakovsky Park. If you cannot feel that, comrade, I cannot help you.

Peter: But . . . the pieces fall, building a ziggurat, all full of gaps and holes, stretching into that empty sky.

Daniel: *As Alexey Pajitnov.* Instinct may tell you that good puzzles can only be solved through the application of great thought. But, so few of us are great thinkers, comrade, so I shall tell you this: The best puzzles are those in which the answer is already self-evident.

Silence. Peter makes a move on the chessboard.

Daniel: . . . Your hand shakes like that, sometimes.

Peter: . . . Yeah, it does.

Daniel: How come?

Peter: . . . I don't know, I see things—visions, I guess—and when I do, my hand twitches . . . Helps me keep track of what's real and what's isn't.

Daniel: Mmn . . .

Peter: I like to think that it's searching for something . . .

Daniel: For what?

Peter: I don't know. Something it lost along the way, I guess . . .

Silence.

Peter: My psychologist says I need to reach out to people more . . . Says I don't have enough human contact . . . He's right, too, that's the stupid thing. Even with him, we have our sessions in a chat room on the 'net. I've never even heard his voice. For all I know, he doesn't even have one.

Silence.

Daniel: I'm from out east. Ontario. My uncle had a ham radio in the shed an' we'd sit out there, playin' chess and list'nin' to voices punch through the static. He was on disability and spent most of his time with that ham, talkin' to the truckers passin' through. I don't think they ever met but when he died, there were all these strangers at his funeral, too choked up to say a word.

Peter: I don't think my psychologist would make it for a funeral. . . .

Silence.

Daniel: Miss my uncle sometimes. Bank came and took his trailer an' ev'ryone fought over who got to pawn the ham . . . I couldn' take that shit, so I snuck into the shed one night an' folded up the chess set an' jus' . . . jus' left . . . By the time win'er settled in, I'd hitched it all the way from Hamilton to Edmonton an' I guess I jus' haven' left here yet. . . . Every now and then, I think I see one of those choked-up strangers walkin' by. I watch for 'em, now, tell myself not to hit 'em up for change—

Peter: Little snippets of my life—

Daniel: —'ey've prob'ly given enough, I figure.

Peter: —strung together with electrical tape and visions and images of myself reflected in a stranger's face, all refracted by the light.

Silence.

Peter: *To Daniel.* A while back, I bought a computer game called The Sims and unwrapped the brightly-coloured box on my way home. In it, you create a character and build a house for him. You buy him furniture and fish tanks. You tell him when to go to the washroom, when to go to bed, when to use the computer, whether or not to look for a job. And meanwhile the neighbours come over every now and then to talk about UFOs, play a little game of chess together, chat about the lawn.

But the game has this dark underbelly, you see? You can build a house with no windows and no doors. You can wall off the bathroom, sell the fridge, shoot the lights. You can tell his friends to stop calling. Little by little, you can drive your Sim mad . . . Sim-torture . . .

Daniel: Peter . . .

Peter: *Not hearing him.* And then, one day, you step back and realize with horror what it is you're doing. Frantic, you install a door, you throw in some windows, you let him see the sky again! You tell yourself it's just a stupid game yet you do everything you can to piece together the shambles of the life you've taken from him.

Daniel: Peter . . .

Peter: *Not hearing him.* And you feel guilty each time you quit playing because a part of you wishes you could reach out to that Sim and tell him that you're sorry . . . you didn't mean for it to be like this. . . .

Daniel: Peter, it's time . . .

Peter: God?

Daniel: No, man, it's Daniel. You . . . You sorta zoned out there for a bit.

Peter: Yeah?

Daniel: Didn' wanna disturb you, but the café opened mebbe five minutes ago. . . .

Peter: Maybe I'll just stay here and try to get a little sleep.

Daniel: All right . . .

SCENE THREE: NOVEMBER

Outside the café. Night. Peter and Daniel both sleep beside the café door, curled together against the cold, the chess set still in play before them. As they sleep, Deep Blue offers up a benediction.

Blue: The message we bring you now is not our own. We built it from YOUR words, the words of a gifted and a lonely people. We placed them in a bottle for you that someday you might find them and hold them dear:

Celebrate the beauty of your impermanence. And when

you search for us, remember that you are searching for yourself. Because, above all, you must love one another, deeply and without reserve. For you are not dead here yet and the space between you is not uncrossable. . . .

Peter is woken by the benediction's closing words. He disentangles himself from Daniel as he speaks, careful not wake him.

Peter: I wake up to the sound of distant waves and the shimmer of the northern lights. Something in me can still hear the distant voice and feel the vaporous breath that forms its parting benediction . . .

But behind me, the café is open early. I enter and sit there, numb. There is no high, no rush.

The lines of Dr. Weizenbaum are once again projected against an upstage screen.

Weizen: Hello, Peter.

Peter: Hello, Dr. Weizenbaum.

Weizen: Shall we begin?

Peter: Can we talk about Daniel?

Weizen: Can you clarify that a bit?

Peter: He sleeps outside the café.

Weizen: I see.

Peter: He's honest and calm. I find him comforting.

Weizen: I'm not sure I know what you're talking about.

Peter: Remember the time you told me I need to reach out to people more?

Weizen: Oh, I told you you need to reach out to people more?

Peter: Yes. Don't you remember?

Weizen: You are sure?

Peter: Of course I'm sure!

Weizen: How long have you been sure?

Peter: I said I wanted to talk about Daniel!

Weizen: What does that suggest to you?

Peter: It suggests that you're not listening to me!

Weizen: Does it please you to believe I am not listening to you?

Peter: Yes, all right? It makes me happy. It makes me happy to know that no one out there is listening to me!

Weizen: And?

Peter: That no one out there is listening to me and—and that I haven't touched a single person's life and made it—and made it meaningful, somehow.

Weizen: You are being a bit negative.

Peter: Yes, I'm being a bit negative. What does that suggest to you?

Silence.

Daniel: *As Garry Kasparov.* You see, my friend? You understand? The space between us cannot be crossed. People in future generations will look back and say THIS was the moment when it all unravelled. It's only a matter of time: The clock is ticking . . . We're dead here, now.

Peter: No, Garry. We're not.

Daniel: *As Garry Kasparov.* What do YOU know, anyway? You talk to visions.

Silence.

Peter: Yeah. I do.

Garry exits the café, broken.

Peter: And in this silent, voiceless place, I felt the need for sun, for air, for space . . .

Peter exits the café, rejoining Daniel who is pondering his next move. He makes it as Peter approaches, capturing his last remaining piece besides the king.

Daniel: See that one, there? It's a poplar, the last to lose its leaves each year . . . Some of them never fall off at all and rustle like old newspaper until spring.

Peter: It's just waiting, isn't it?

Daniel: Yeah.

Peter: So what if spring never comes? What if everything just keeps getting colder and colder until the world just sort of ends?

Daniel: I dunno.

Peter: No?

Daniel: I don' think anythin' really ever ends.

Silence.

Daniel: Things have this rhythm, see? Always movin', always changin' . . . An endin' is just when those things become somethin' we hadn't been expectin'.

Peter: Something we hadn't been expecting, eh?

Daniel: Yeah, like that computer guy you talk to. Did he start out tryin' to do what he ended up doin' or did it just sorta happen along the way?

Peter: I—I don't know.

Daniel: *As David Cope.* I first created Emmy when I was suffering from a fairly bad case of composer's block in my own work . . . But then I started feeding it pieces of Bach, of Mozart, of Rachmaninoff. I felt guilty, like a priest committing theft and sacrilege amongst the dead.

Peter: Maybe our finest moments are always crafted from despair . . . and it's only while we're in such a vulnerable state that those moments can overtake us with all the power of their beauty.

Daniel: *As David Cope.* Maybe Picasso was onto something when he said "Good painters borrow, great painters steal . . ." Maybe nothing we create is entirely our own. When we go back and look at music in scattered fragments as Emmy does, we see that Beethoven, Mozart, they all borrowed from other composers. Perhaps creative genius lies not in spinning a whole new tapestry but in diligently stitching together a patchwork quilt from scraps at hand.

Peter: Can't we live our lives with equal genius, piecing together our patchwork worlds from photographs and voices and the memories of things? Emmy and Aaron, they're just trying to teach us something about being human, about keeping that art in the background always changing, always new, always forbidden. We can do it that way, can't we?

Daniel: *As Alexey Pajitnov.* So few of us are great thinkers, comrade, so I shall tell you this:

Peter: *To Alexey.* "The best puzzles are those in which the answer is already self-evident?" . . .But what if we don't like the answers we've been given?

Daniel: *As Alexey Pajitnov.* Success in Tetris lies somewhere between your reflexes and your reason. You must understand the structure as a whole but still bear witness to the individual pieces and their relations to one another. Their shapes are easy to memorize and recognize but you must make your decisions. In a short while, comrade, you will find that it has become an ingrained and automatic part of you.

Silence.

Peter: *To God.* God.

Silence.

Peter: I don't know if you can hear me anymore . . .

Silence.

Peter: But I wanted to tell you that, even if the world is ending . . . I've been happy here.

Silence. Peter moves to the chessboard and tips over his own king.

Daniel: Checkmate.

Silence.

Peter: *To Daniel.* We reach out . . .

Daniel: *To Peter.* and touch nothing.

Peter: We scan the stars . . .

Daniel: and find the edge of time.

Peter: We send our best and brightest to the moon . . .

Daniel: to bring back dust.

Peter: There is an infinite space inside us. It is what makes us such a gifted and a lonely people; what makes us always fly so far beneath that deep blue sky.

Daniel: Little snippets of our lives, strung together with electrical tape and visions and the terrible, undeniable knowledge—

Peter: —that we are alone in the universe.

Silence.

Peter: Daniel?

Daniel: Yeah?

Peter: Tell me about your family.

Daniel: I dunno. Never had a dad. My mom and I lived at my uncle's. You come from a big family?

Peter: Three sisters, all older. I was the youngest by a good seven years. By the time I hit university, two of them had already moved west to BC and the other had married a fellow down in the States. . . . Dad died of a heart attack when I was in university and Mom of grief eight months later.

Daniel: . . . How were the funerals?

Peter: All right, I guess. Did the job. They left me enough to live off of, for now at least. Guess it'll run out someday.

Daniel: You can stay with me if you wanna. . . .

Peter: Yeah . . .

Silence.

Peter: I had access to the Internet at the university. Nothing fancy, just text. Didn't seem like much at all, really, not like we have now . . . But then I stumbled across this site with a program called Eliza. You'd type in stuff to her and she'd build questions out of it. She'd use diversionary tactics to deflect attention away from herself, and she drew on a bunch of stock phrases whenever she encountered something she couldn't understand.

Daniel: What was she like?

Peter: When she was created way back in 1966, she was given the personality of a Rogerian psychotherapist. Her creator . . . his name was Joseph Weizenbaum.

Silence.

Peter: Hello, Eliza.

Dr. Weizenbaum's lines are projected against the upstage screen one last time.

Weizen: How do you do. Please state your problem.

Peter: When I was nineteen, I bought a bone-white Cessna and I flew away from everything I'd ever known.

Weizen: I'm not sure I know what you're talking about.

Peter: You tucked a message into a bottle, and tied it to my fuselage.

Weizen: Can you elaborate on that?

Peter: I've opened it, now, and I've read it and it says "We are not dead here yet. The space between us is not uncrossable."

Weizen: What does that suggest to you?

Peter: I think I have found everything I needed here.

Weizen: But you are not sure you have found everything you needed here?

Peter: Goodbye, Dr. Weizenbaum.

Weizen: Please go on.

Peter: Goodbye, Eliza.

Weizen: Please go on.

Peter: I'll miss you both. . . .

Weizen: Please go on.

Silence.

Daniel: Peter?

Peter: Yeah?

Daniel: Why do you sit outside here with me?

Peter: I like to hear you talk.

Daniel: Hmn. You like to hear yourself talk.

Peter: That's true, too. Hey, it beats playing against myself.

Daniel: You gonna keep comin' back?

Peter: I think so.

Daniel: I'd like that.

Peter: . . . It's getting cold. Should we go grab some coffee from the bus station?

Daniel: No. Let's just stay here for a while.

Peter: . . . All right.

Long silence. Daniel curls up and goes to sleep. Peter begins setting up the chessboard for another game.

Peter: And on the doorstep of the Internet café, it is already twilight. There are no clouds for miles but that doesn't stop the snow from forming between the layers of the deep blue sky. It's fine, like moondust by which we trace the outlines of things . . . It is the middle of November, so temporary, so transient, and yet so all-embracing. In the grace of an unseen God, there sleeps a man named Daniel, covered up by newspaper and moondust and by the rustling of the poplar leaves. He looks dead . . . but he's just waiting.

END

Back Row: Cresh (Jon Stewart), Tubix (Kevin Jesuino), Morelle (Trish Lorenz). Front Row: Tilly (Vincent Forcier) in *Grumplestock's*.

Grumplestock's

Kevin Jesuino,
Trish Lorenz,
Jon Stewart

My first encounter with *Grumplestock's* was quite incidental. After the trio of writers had abandoned a rushed plan to present the play independently at Azimuth Theatre in December of 2004, Trish Lorenz gave me a copy of the script. At that time I was unable to read it beginning to end but I flipped through a few pages to see what was going on. What I encountered in my idle perusal was a very playful and engaging sense of language. So I ensured that the creators had Nextfest on their radar and left it in anticipation of the time when I would get to sit down and properly ingest it. When that time came, I was not disappointed. Not only did the script possess a playful style, cadence, and meaning, but also a story that does what I think theatre is supposed to do: present the audience with a vision of themselves.

The act of watching contemporary theatre often feels to me like going to the zoo. A lot of effort is expended creating the illusion that we are engaged in the study of the natural world, yet practically everything is artificial. An air of danger is desirable but there is no real risk whatsoever. Creatures are observed pacing about an enclosed space and occasionally one remarks on the similarity between the low behaviours of the observed and the higher behaviours of the observer. There is an unchallenged assumption that the object of the observation is something less than human. The theatre audience and the zoo audience are both cast in the role of the inactive voyeur. So, when a play comes my way that implicates the audience and turns the space between the audience and the performance from a peephole into a mirror, I get excited. *Grumplestock's* is the kind of play that puts the audience on stage.

Grumplestock's has a clear and unified thematic core, which I find remarkable for a play written by three minds. This is mostly due to it being built upon a very decided proposal from its initiator, Kevin Jesuino. Following is Kevin's original journal entry that sparked the whole enterprise:

Grumplestock's Travelling Mad Marionettes Show

There's a moment every night when the marionettes of Grumplestock's Travelling Marionettes Show come to life. For over two hundred years this has been occurring, as the marionettes come to life and perform for the people. How do they come to life, you may ask? Well, many people do not know the secret to Grumplestock's Travelling Marionettes because soon after their show is done for the evening, old Grumplestock packs his marionettes away in the travelling wagon and moves onto the next city. For two hundred years he's been raking in the money from people who want to see the life-like marionettes. He drinks his own ever-lasting potion to keep him living. But the marionettes are tired of being controlled by Grumplestock. But how will they continue to live with out Grumplestocks' magic? Magic and an uprising of mad marionettes are about to overtake Grumplestock's Travelling Marionettes Show.

—Kevin Jesuino, August 2004

Based on this nugget, the three conspirators discussed and physically explored their way to four marionettes, each endowed with a particular emotion and a flaw arising from their deepest desires. Then they applied themselves to the creation of text that would tell the several adventures of Grumplestock's Mad Marionettes. They then invited Vince Forcier into the mix to interpret the role of Tilly.

Facilitating this particular production at Nextfest was problematic. The fact that there were three co-authhours who were also going to be performing in it was not the least of the difficulties but neither was it the greatest. At the time of the first rehearsal one of the actors was still in Europe, one had just arrived from Vancouver, the Stage Manager and Designer were strangers to the rest, and the Director was in Toronto. I have to confess to being somewhat invasive (though confess suggests I feel guilt and remorse—which I do not) in the process of curating this project. So when the team started to feel trepidation at not being able to have a show ready that they could be proud of in time for the Festival, I was . . . "insistent" would be the most complimentary term to describe my reaction. One could also say "pushy." Sometimes pushing kids in the water is the best way to make them swim.

The Nextfest production of *Grumplestock's* was clean and sharp under Aaron Mackenzie's choreographed direction. Transitions between characters and realities were delivered through bold physical characterizations and assisted by equally bold costume contributions from Snezana Pesic. The set consisted of four large, yet mobile boxes and a painted backdrop of Bowble that reinforced the idea that these marionettes were themselves theatrical contrivances breathing in a theatrical atmosphere.

– S.P.

PRODUCTION HISTORY

Grumplestock's was first presented at nextfest 2005 at the Roxy Theatre with the following team:

Morelle: *Trish Lorenz*
Tubix: *Kevin Jesuino*
Cresh: *Jon Stewart*
Tilly: *Vincent Forcier*
Director: *Aaron MacKenzie*
Designer: *Snezana Pesic*
Stage Manager: *Maggie McCaw*

This production continued on to The 2005 Edmonton Fringe A-Go-Go later that summer at the Cosmopolitan Music Society (8426–103 Street) where they worked without a Director making only minor changes to Aaron's blocking. They had to say farewell to some of the costume elements that were borrowed for the Nextfest production, so new pieces had to be created and Jon's mom was instrumental in the construction of new costumes. Here's to mothers. The production team remained the same with the following changes and additions:

Stage Manager: *Shayla Bander*
Backstage Tech: *Leah Doz*

CHARACTERS

Morelle: A motherly ballerina who craves love.
Tubix: A gentleman of aristocratic bearing and straight lines.
Cresh: A brat, an imp.
Tilly: A sack of sadness sighing through life's aching.

The play's title refers to the four principal characters above. They are marionettes but are played by human actors. These four characters, being performers, take on the task of presenting all other characters in their story who are—with the exception of Grumplestock—residents of Bowble. Bowble is organized by a rigid caste system that consists of the following groups:

Carkers: Market folk guided by the morality of profit.

Suples: Lowest caste, homeless, poor as poor, dirty as dirt.

Knockentalks: The uppermost class, corrupt, loud, boors.

Slips: Prostitutes stabled primarily for the pleasure of Knockentalks.

Glimmers: Punishing night sprits, like flying razor blades.

Grumplestock: A maker and manipulator of marionettes. Depicted in chorus by all four.

Guard: Guards the gate of Bowble, played by Tilly.

Gramaphone Lady: A crackling mystic, played by Cresh.

Cartsmen Stynhart: A charmer, a violinist, a manager of a brothel, a procurer of Slips, played by Tubix.

Merchant: A Carker, played by Tubix.

Grittle: A particularly sinister Carker with a vendetta for Cartsmen Stynhart, played by Tilly.

Dark Man: Grittle's henchmen, played by Morelle.

Fabious Montagory: A Knockentalk, played by Cresh.

Suples 1, 2, 3: Played by Morelle, Tubix and Cresh.

Knockentalks 1,2: Played by Morelle and Tilly.

Countess: A leader in Bowble's Knockentalk community, played by Morelle.

Slips 1,2: Played by Cresh and Tilly.

SETTING

A box used to store four marionettes. A road leading to Bowble. Various locations in the town of Bowble.

Grumplestock's

No light. In the darkness, whispering. "Nothing but magic." "Do you know Grumplestock?" etc. One ray of light from the ceiling appears downstage centre. Slowly, we see the faces of the four marionettes flicker by in the light. The whispering rises to a climax, then stops. No sound.

All: No space . . . no feeling. No room. No light, but for a shred. No friends. Only magic. Only magic. Only us.

The lights come up, but only slightly. It is still difficult to see the features of the marionettes.

Voices:

Two voices prominent.

Too many feelings
All at once
This is the horror
This is the consequence
Of being human

Two voices in a whisper.

under the earth
nothing left
nothing but magic
nothing but magic
no space

All: Has he left us? Have we been naughty? Has Grumplestock left his kiddies?

Voices:

Two voices.

Grumplestock?
Yes, Grumplestock.
No really?
Yes
No!
Yes
A bear of a man?
YES!
Strong, and wise

Two voices.

He's coming

He's here now

He's looking

He's looking
Looking for
His children

All: And they say he has magic!

Voices:

Two voices.

Magic!

Two voices.

Too much

No!
Yes, magic!   Only magic
Really?
Yes!   Enough to stop time
No!
YES!
But NOT TRICKS

All: Real magic, to blow your mind in four directions!

Tubix: We belong to him.

Morelle: We are his.

All: We are Grumplestock's.

Tubix: And no one else's . . .

Cresh: He's found us . . .

Tilly: Have we been bad?

Tubix: It's where we belong, friends.

All: Better than out there . . .

Beat.

All: Ohhh . . . Hello there. You found us.

Cresh: Are you listening?

Tilly: This is important.

Tubix: Friends . . . our story is ready I think.

Tilly: Our story?

Cresh: Yes, at long last!

Morelle: It's truly magnificent.

Cresh: Look for that magic. Because that is what truly makes a story.

Tilly: A story . . . oh, yes.

All: But to finally tell one of our own . . .

Tubix: It is common fact that marionettes are expert storytellers. And do we have one for you!

All: *Slowly.* No space, no light, no space, no light . . .

Voices:

Two voices.
No space no light . . .
No space no light . . .

Two voices.
Nothing but magic . . .
Nothing but magic . . .

Two voices.   *One voice.*   *One voice.*
No space no light . . .   Nothing but magic . . .   One single sliver
No space no light . . .   Nothing but magic . . .   of HOPE . . .

All: NOTHING BUT THE STORY . . . BREATHE IT IN . . .

They breathe. They open their eyes.

All: This is our story. We are his. We are Grumplestock's.

Still in a light whisper.

Cresh: How did we begin?

Tubix: How were we born?

Morelle: Where did our life come from?

Tilly: *Slowly.* We . . . were . . . a . . . show!

All: A SHOW!

The lights explode up, music plays and the marionettes begin to dance. As they speak, individually, the others continue the dance upstage.

Tubix: But not any show. Everyone would come to see ours. We were dancers, singers, performers, and boy we were damn good too. The secret to our show wasn't just the moving, the dancing, in fact, that's not why they came . . .

Cresh and Morelle advance.

Cresh: They came . . . yes they came for what they call—

Morelle: Magic!

The music and dance comes to a slow motion.

Cresh: MAGIC . . . they were in awe by the simple wave of a hand . . .

Morelle: Grumplestock . . . MADE us . . . from magic. To see us move, speak, sing, dance, blink, even BREATHING was a miracle.

Tilly: They called us walking miracles . . . old Grumplestock made us his miracle marionettes.

A shift—the puppets move to re-enact their birth. Music cross fades to a new melody. Tilly comes forward.

Tilly: Miracles in each stroke . . . our lives were branded with velvet paint. Souls were built like sticks and glue . . . but laced with wonders . . . and wound gently around one single emotion . . .

Tubix: In simple, educated terms . . . the magic only worked to create a single, focused energy . . .

Tilly: And so . . . strokepaintbrush . . . and it was made:

All: MORELLE

Morelle: *Advancing* Morelle. Painted with the flutter of inno-cence, and the wide-eyed posture of curiosity.

Tilly: strokepaintbrush:

All: TUBIX

Tubix: Tubix. Pomp and posture, presentation. Knowledge is power, and power is popularity!

Tilly: strokepaintbrush:

All: CRESH

Cresh: Playful and quick, smiles and laughs make your life a bash.

Tilly: strokepaintbrush—

All: strokepaintbrush: TILLY

Tilly: Tilly. What do you do when your life begins and ends in an endless pit. No smile. No sunlight. No cheers. Nothing but Tilly. Nothing but a withered heart, and the end before it's ever begun.

Cresh: We were the greatest, most wonderful puppets ever seen!

Tilly: We were made for that. We were made to tell stories. Always to entertain.

All: AND WE DID!!!

Morelle: Through Morowville, up the greenlands, through the mountains, oh dear, stop in the corner of Zatras, that's a shifty one performing, and travellingtravellingtravelling dance-dancedance travellingtravellingtravelling, no rest, TIRED—

Others: BREAAAAAAK!

Morelle: It was a great time.

Cresh: It was a nightmare!

Morelle: We saw the world!

Tubix: I saw Cresh vomit. . . .

Tilly: I was sooo tired. . . .

The energy slows.

All: We thought we knew them . . .

Tilly: We THOUGHT we knew.

Tubix: But what we learned astounded us all.

Cresh: When a crack of the world's light is set upon fresh minds . . . mischief will arise . . . and deeds will be done . . . and with great knowledge also comes a certain consequence . . .

Morelle: We came . . . one day . . .

All: To leave our show . . . and to leave our father, Grumplestock. . . .

They sit still. They are in the wagon. They rock and rear, as the wagon tumbles along. Silence.

Cresh: THAT GRUMPLESTOCK!

Others: SHHHH!

Pause.

Tubix: He's our father, Cresh.

Cresh: Ha! To keep us here . . .

Morelle: Best be quiet—

Tilly: Cresh, don't speak like that.

Morelle: Come now! Shh!

Tilly: Please!

Quiet as they rock.

Cresh: Tilly . . . such a weakling! Always with Tubix—

Tubix: Now that's enough, you barbarian!

A great bump. The four sit quietly, and stare . . . then are relieved. They laugh a bit, and silently forgive each other with a look. Suddenly, another great rock, and the sound of the cart collapsing ensues. Then, silence.

Tubix: The rest of them were afraid. But I knew exactly what had happen—the crate had grown legs. Eventually everything grows legs, and at that moment it grew its legs and threw itself off the wagon. And, although I assumed, through calculations and meticulous formulas, that it was going to occur much later in time, it decided to do so prematurely. And so here we are. Away from Grumplestock and alone.

Nobody worry, I have this all under control. Now, let me find my highly sensitive where-to-go-locator. *Pulls out a pocket watch.* Now you see, the big hand is pointing that way, and the small hand is pointing that way . . . therefore, it means we walk . . . uhm . . . that way.

Cresh: That's a pocket watch.

Morelle: Where did you get that?

Tubix: I discovered its effects upon our performance in Gabion's Crest. Ever since, the device has aided me in all of my travels and adventures.

Tilly: Well you've NEVER been away . . .

Cresh: How do you know it works?

Tubix: I'm sure of its enchanting luck and powers . . . my performance that day was wonderful . . . even more so than as per usual . . . I was filled with such Vlave!

Morelle: Vlave isn't a word!

Tubix: Of course it is. Look it up the dictionary that I'm writing. Look, my highly sensitive where-to-go-locater is telling us that we need to go. Whatever is over that way is meant to have us.

Tilly: I don't want to be had by anything!

Morelle: What do you suppose is over there?

Tubix: I don't know. That's why it's telling us to get there. So, we could stand here, lost, and completely useless to ourselves, or we could begin to walk in some direction and take whatever comes to us. Now are you with me?

Cresh: This will not end well. . . .

A shift of light or sound.

Tilly/Cresh: And now we journey . . .

Tubix/Morelle: . . . on for some time . . .

Tilly/Cresh: . . . over hillsides, rocks, mountains,
Plains, on and on, never stopping
Tired beyond ourselves,
On and on and on and . . .

They stop.

Cresh: And suddenly . . .

All: THERE IT WAS. THE ORANGE FORTRESS.

Morelle: A castle of incomprehensible size. A shadowed city.

Tubix: A city in hiding.

Cresh: Bowble . . . a city of extremes.

Tubix: This happens to be the true wonder of our story.

Cresh: And we will be playing every man woman and creature in the city of Bowble.

Morelle: We will play all the parts.

All: So keep with us . . . *Looking up to the city.* Here we are.

They arrive to see the guard.

Tubix: Ladies and gentlemen, our destination.

Tilly: They have very high walls.

Tubix: Now don't be afraid Tilly . . . we'll be safe!

Tilly: *Weeping.* Ohooo . . . *Hides away from them.*

Cresh: Little pest, always afraid of—

Tilly has become the Bowble guard.

Guard: Halt—your importance in the city of Bowble?

Cresh: Importance . . . thank you.

Guard: What is your duty?

Morelle: We are entertainers!

Guard: And your importance in the city of Bowble?

Cresh: I'm worth twice the importance. Thank you, thank you!

Tubix: I believe he wants to know what we are doing here. Let me have at him. Sir, we merely seek a place to rest.

Guard: Be that your only reason to visit the city of Bowble?

Tubix: . . . yes.

Guard: Proceed at your own risk.

Tubix: Unkindly little badger isn't he?

Tilly: Is he gone?

Cresh: Yes . . . the bad man is gone! You can stop shedding tears, and continue living your little life again. Now what type of city is called "Bowble"?

Tubix: What type of puppet is called "Cresh"?

Cresh: You're looking for some, Tubix!

Morelle: Stop it, you two!

Cresh: Fine, I don't even care!

Tubix: Quiet now! Best to focus on what's right in front of us.

The Gramaphone Lady appears.

Grama: Do you know when the next full moon is?

Morelle: Hello, Miss.

Grama: Do you know when the next full moon is?

Morelle: Full moon? I'm sorry, I don't understand you.

Tilly: The moon. *Points to the sky.* Except fuller. Prettier.

Grama: Yes! Do you know when it's coming?

Tilly: I do not. Sorry.

Grama: Bah . . . Full moon. Midnight. Chatamaphagory Manor.

Morelle: What's happening there?

Grama: Chatamaphagory Manor. Full moon. Midnight. Be there and you'll find out. OH! I've made an error, a mistake. P-p-p-p-pardon for the coloring of your type, but you four seem different from everyone around here. An unexpected pleasance among a soup of shadows. I haven't smiled like this in ages.

Tilly: What do you mean?

Grama: Don't you understand the word? DIFFERENT! But you four cannot yet understand. It is too early in the c-c-c-cycles of life span across the sky, let me let me let me let me let me out! DIFFERENT DIFFERENT, a new age.

Tubix: Slow down please!

Grama: Bowble! Are we awake yet? You've arrived my pleasant puppy puppets. Hello! Let me spread some light on Bowble. Light light LIGHT Moonlight! Don't forget, Chatamaphagory Manor.

Full moon. Midnight. Not enough time now. By then, you'll have discovered your importance here. Always look for your importance, my little pud-muffins. Must find one's purpose that night.

No time nonono RUN the hour is near. Keep quiet in a safe place where you can rest for the night. Darkness comes to these parts of Bowble. That brings out the pesky Glimmers.

Morelle: Glimmers?

Grama: The fairies of the night. Always one step ahead of the sun's front. Living in shadow—robbing from anyone that is left past the glow of the moon. The flies of judgement in Bowble's black heart. There's too much sin for them to tell the difference and that means YOU'RE NEXT. Quickly. Quickly. Quickly. Quickly. The city of Bowble is closing its eyes. The sound of wings approach!

She exits, becoming Cresh once more.

Tilly: What a strange woman. . . .

Tubix: A nuisance if you ask me . . . complete bother really!

Cresh: What did she mean . . . importance?

Morelle: She said that we're here to make ourselves important. Find what we are. Now, what about those Glimmers?

Tubix: Morelle, it's a simple fable, a lie made up to scare people from this wretched town.

Cresh: Tubix, you don't know anything! What's to say that this woman was wrong?

Tubix: What did you say to me?

Tilly: Um . . . we shouldn't fight . . .

Cresh: Shouldn't fight, Tilly?

Morelle: I think I hear something . . .

Tubix: *to Cresh.* Who made you leader?	**Cresh:** *to Tilly.* Why are you so puny?	**Morelle:** I hear . . .
Cresh: *to Tubix.* Me leader? Better than you Tubix!	**Tilly:** *to Cresh.* Well I'm sorry— *To both.* Please stop!	**Morelle:** There's . . . Quiet . . . Quiet!!
Tubix: *to Cresh.* Someone should box you, Cresh . . .	**Cresh:** *to Tubix.* Come now, Look where we are!	**Tilly:** *to himself.* Ohhhh!

Cacophony builds to this point.

Morelle: QUIET! QUIET!

Morelle: Do you hear that, friends . . . do you hear what's coming?

All: And there came the beautiful and sharp, striking Glimmers . . . SPIRITS OF THE BOWBLE NIGHT, the nightmares come at inhuman speeds, and there STRIKE!

Tilly: Tubix! Help me! They hurt! They sting, they burn!

Tubix: I'm coming Tilly! OH! Ahhhhh! Morelle?! Cresh!

Cresh: Quickly along fellows! Find shelter!

Morelle: RUN! RUN! THEY'LL KILL US!

All: Fly away . . . run for your life . . . nightmares always a nose behind.

Morelle: Tubix, I see a house!

Tubix: Hurry, it's just up ahead!

All: Sting, snap, sharp, one nose behind, THERE'S THE HOUSE, sting, snap, sharp, one nose behind, close the door, close the door, close the door, CLOSE THE DOOR!

They escape, slamming the door of the building. They have entered the brothel house. As they close the door, the lights dim. They breathe heavily, and look around, and to each other.

Tilly: Tubix, where are we?

Tubix: I'll tell you in a minute.

Cresh: He doesn't know, you fool. We're lost. As usual. As always. Trapped in a tight spot because of this idiot!

Morelle: Best be quiet, Cresh. We don't know this place.

Tubix: You—I dislike you sometimes, Cresh!

Cresh: *Feigning hurt.* Ohhh you're hurting my feelings!

Cartsmen Stynhart appears. Tubix becomes this character. He plays the violin.

Tilly: Oh my.

Cresh: You. You! We need help.

Stynhart: Good evening. Newcomers to Bowble I suppose.

Tilly: Yes. Sorry . . . But it's a vicious, awful night . . . and there are creatures outside.

Stynhart: Every night is as such. You should get used to the feeling of fear.

Cresh: Well we need a place to rest, sir!

Stynhart sees Morelle, and approaches her, ignoring the others.

Stynhart: You seem very familiar . . . I know you somehow.

Morelle: Excuse me?

Stynhart: So incredibly vibrant . . . I feel like I know you. . . . *Pausing, and keeping his eyes on Morelle.* There are beds down the hall. And ignore anything you see in your chambers. Each bed is just as filthy as the next one.

Cresh and Tilly go off. Morelle begins to leave.

Stynhart: You, stay. Please .

Morelle: Thank you, sir. But I don't even know you.

Stynhart: But of course! I am Cartsmen Stynhart. Known very well here in Bowble. Respected gentleman of sophisticated business.

Pause.

Stynhart: Normally when one is introduced, the other should say her name as well.

Morelle: Oh . . . my name is Morelle.

Stynhart: Morelle. An absolute pleasure. I can't forget a name like that, can I? Come. Sit. Let's get to know one another better.

Morelle: What is it that you do after all?

Stynhart: I guess you could say that I deal with public relations. Plain, and simple, dearest Morelle. I own Slips. I sell them. They please the men of this city and during the night, the skies and mist fill with the drawn sounds of pleasure and wetness, and then they come back to me . . . under my spell. *Pause.*

Morelle: Oh. I see.

He moves closer and touches her face. Morelle retreats.

Stynhart: My dear, please forgive me. I mean you no harm. It's just that . . . Morelle, you are such a wondrous piece of work!

Morelle: Yes, sir. I was made this way.

Stynhart: Why, yes. I suppose you were!

He picks up his violin and begins to play.

Morelle: Your violin is magical.

Stynhart: Possibly the greatest piece of magic in Bowble. It brings out the soul of my creatures.

Morelle: Where did you learn to play?

She begins to move to the violin's music.

Stynhart: *Laughing* Well! Quite curious, aren't you? *He pauses for a moment, then continues in a serious manner.* My mother taught me. She used to play for me. She carved this violin from a piece of wood. With her own two hands. Her love was so strong, she said, so powerful that only we could understand it. Just a simple piece of wood and yet such beauty . . . Such power and magic . . .

He continues to play as Morelle dances. He watches. Stynhart plays his violin as she lies down, he stays, as the other two speak.

All: Grumplestock?
Yes Grumplestock!
HERE?
Here!
In Bowble.
Looking for his children.
GRUMPLESTOCK IS HERE.

Tubix: *As himself.* Good morning, everyone!

Tilly: Good morning, Tubix.

Cresh: Where did that man go?

Morelle: He left.

Tubix: What did he say to you, Morelle?

Cresh: Forget the man! Look at this day!

Tilly: It is fairly pretty. . . .

Tubix: Now be careful, the streets of this place are probably the most dangerous—*Cresh scampers off.* CRESH, DON'T RUN OFF!

The Gramaphone lady appears in another triumphant surprise.

Grama: Do you know when the next full moon is?

Morelle: Hello again!

Grama: Chatamaphagory Manor, midnight. Importance. I must apologize. Sometimes one's behavior makes behaving quite evasive, yes? I may have seemed desperate once before, but . . . it is only because you four seem so promising. But perhaps my pupils and mind lie to the truth of the matter. In short . . . your purpose here in the city . . . is to DISCOVER your purpose. Discover this, and you'll know why you are important. But, for now, my new arrivals, I'm here to give you the grand tour!

Tubix: We're not sure that we can afford to go along with that. Our friend just ran ahead, and—

Morelle: Cresh will be fine, Tubix. Let's just follow this nice lady.

Grama: The little bitch is right . . . let's get the grama going . . . just like this . . . there we go, HERE is the city of Bowble!

Morelle: Why are they so dark?

Grama: Because, little pipsy, the Slips have nowhere else to go. Their mind is rotating around and around itself. Quite sad isn't it, but don't frighten yourself. They were meant to be that way.

Now we're getting into some nasty territory . . . into the market . . . this is where the Carkers live.

Tilly: Carkers?

Grama: Market folk. They sell everything they own. Just keep your money to yourselves.

Tilly: What money?

They pass some Suples.

Tilly: Oh dear. Who are they?

Grama: Those . . . those are the Suples.

Suple 1: Help me . . . help me up.

Suple 2: Do you have any coin?

Tilly: I'm sorry . . .

Grama: Ignore them. You can't help the Suples. They are always falling, and never getting up. They were born that way. As they are, Knockentalks beat them for being poor.

Give them money, and the Knockentalks beat them harder for not being poor enough. Don't stare.

Tubix: Who are the Knockentalks?

Grama: The upperclassmen. Gamblers and tyrants, who live for nothing but to be everything. They sit, and produce fame and glamour . . . black and white politicians, feasting on those lower than themselves, and bringing this corrupted city lower and lower. And there you have it. Bowble. And that's all you need to know.

Morelle: You've been very kind.

Tilly: Bye-bye!

Grama: Bye-bye . . . bye bye bye bye bye bye BYE!? If that's all that you can state, your proposed response NEEDS IMPROVEMENT. For never neglect my prophesy to you. The winds of change must be felt. And sometimes, it is irrelevant to begin simply waiting for them. Listen to my words . . . please. They may be staggered, confusing, blurred. Decipher me. Follow my guide. The poison of this city cannot be cured lest it's first exposed. It may be some time before you see me again. Find your place. FIND . . . your purpose. FIND . . . WHY . . . YOU'RE . . . HERE.

They call for Cresh. The Gramaphone Lady disappears.

Tilly: Cresh . . .

Morelle: Cresh?

All Three: CRESH!

A shift. We are brought to where Cresh has left off, scurrying through the market place.

Merchant: Ah! Ah! Grittle Grittle, my head man, my liege . . . my—Good to see you, of course, and you as well, whoever you are, I know it's a broad business! I mean, well, how are you, you know, keeping busy, I saw you out, well, you look wonderful of course, and—

Grittle: Best to quiet down before you shit yourself little man.

Merchant: A-HAAAAA! Yes, um, well, a little nervous of course. First sale to the big Boss, Grittle. I understand that uh . . . you're looking for a special kind of uh, hehehehe, ointment.

Grittle: Well you can speak about it out loud my friend . . . poison is the name of the game. All I need to see is whether you're worth all that people say. Otherwise . . . I have friends that can easily deal with you and your business . . . you'll be as worthless as a Suple.

Dark Man: I'll see to it myself.

Merchant: Oh, no worries, no fear, for see . . . blades, knives, and the deadliest herbs . . . of course if you prefer longer range, there are the most effective darts—

Dark Man: Something a little more subtle . . . something more quiet . . . something to slip into a victim . . .

Merchant: That happens to be my specialty! Sirs, you obviously have not, eh, businessed with this side of the Carkerdom . . . I, unlike many, will not outdo you, not dink you off of sales, you know—

Dark Man: We are lacking in time! *Gentler.* Now, speak . . .

Merchant: You see I am not just some fool. You need quiet murder? Swift vengeance? Because I know the man you wish to kill.

Grittle: Cartsmen Stynhart. It's no secret.

Cresh: *To himself.* Stynhart.

Merchant: Yes, Stynhart, but what folks don't know about the business of death is that Cartsmen Stynhart is invulnerable to many physical and common forms of justice. Only the most potent, powerful enchantments can overcome this man's soul. So much that to kill would only be accessible through his eyes. Those blue windows to his essence . . . and I have it gentlemen. I can make this most important deed come true.

Cresh: *Perking slightly.* Important?

Merchant: I have what has been seemingly extinct since it's brief departure. The brazia orchid—the golden flower.

Dark Man: No!

Merchant: Here she lies. The flower . . . and it's poisonous nectar. Let no one see . . . the golden beauty . . . the soul-stealer . . .

Grittle: Most . . . impressive. . . .

Cresh: *Approaching once again to the shop.* Most . . . important . . .

Cresh approaches the merchant, quickly, dancing and laughing.

Cresh: Ho! I will take that sir! *Taking the flower and its poison.*

Dark Man: A spy!

Merchant: He seeks to stop us!

Cresh: That's a wonderful flower sirs. . . .

Dark Man: . . . This boy must be taught a lesson. . . .

Approaching to grab him.

Cresh: Oh! We play now?

The man is pushed away. The man draws a blade, and swings, as Cresh ducks. Grittle joins in the melee, but is avoided by Cresh.

Merchant: He has the brazia!!!

Dark Man: GET HIM!

A chase ensues through the market.

Grittle: *Grabbing him.* There you go little fellow. I may not look strong, but trust me . . . I am deadlier than any one of these Carkers.

Cresh: Dah! I lost? Well, it was a good game!

Merchant: . . . Kill him Grittle. He stole my poison.

Grittle: Shut it, you fool. What is your name, fellow?

Cresh: . . . Cresh. They call me Cresh.

Grittle: Cresh . . . well . . . you surprise me, little one. Do you work here?

Cresh: No.

Grittle: Do you wish to find something around the Carker centre?

Dark Man: Grittle!

Cresh: *Smiling greatly.* In what direction?

Grittle: In the direction of discovering employment. In becoming of importance to our position.

Cresh: That word again. . . .Yes, sir.

Dark Man: Grittle . . . what are you thinking? It's too late in our plans—

Grittle: *Ignoring the dark man.* You have won the flower, Cresh—you have won respect. But now to win a position of importance. You have already proven that you are useful to our needs. Come back to this spot . . . as the darkness of the city sinks . . . and we will be around to meet you.

Cresh: Well . . . position filled, sir . . . hehehe . . .

Merchant: Nah, nono, I can't stand for losing the brazia! If he understands any of its value, he will not return!

Grittle: And if YOU understand the value of breathing, you'd best accept that sometimes the best business comes from attaining a man willing enough to have his own SPINE! Unlike yourself . . .

Merchant: Ahhhh . . . I will . . . be in touch then. And, eh, thank you, I suppose. For the business. *Cursing.*

Grittle: Be off then. *Signals Dark Man to remove Merchant.* I welcome your company. . . .

Cresh: A pleasure. And joy. *Leaving.*

Grittle: And Cresh . . . bring the nectar with you.

Cresh leaves. Carkers become Morelle and Tubix.

Morelle: CRESH!? Cresh?!

Tubix: Always running off.

Tubix: *Seeing something.* Morelle . . . is that not the man you spoke with?

Morelle: Stynhart?

Cresh becomes Fabious Montagory, and Tubix becomes Cartsmen Stynhart.

Fabious: Pardon the jitters Stynhart, only I worry about this . . .

this is an event of paramount proportions!

Stynhart: I understand the importance, sir. I'll have them brought over just after sundown.

Fabious: Please make sure we get a nice variety—a nice mix, you know.

Stynhart: Thirty-three percent each? Does that sound all right?

Fabious: Yes, yes, just make it a mix. The countess wants one for every guest. None of this double partnering. Keeps it clean this way. And, bring your best. I want our honored guests to have their choice in bests. We've imported the best Gootsap Dip, Macknoy cakes, Dalliops, Cantimope.

Stynhart: Indeed. A variety of my best will arrive at the Federal Tower doors just after sun down. I guarantee no need to be concerned.

Fabious: Thank you, Cartsmen. This will not go unnoticed. *Hands him coins.*

Stynhart: Good day, sir. *Begins to exit, Morelle follows.*

Tubix: Imported Gootsap Dip and Macknoy cakes! Dalliops! Cantimope! A perfect welcoming for a new arrival in Bowble. I hope they don't mind an extra guest at their tables.

Cresh: *Entering.* Tubix! Hello!

Tubix: Cresh! CRESH! WHERE WERE YOU!?

Cresh: *Suspiciously.* Nowhere!

Tubix: You shouldn't run off like that! We must stay together!

Cresh: Well where is Morelle?

Tubix: I'm not sure.

Cresh: Uh—well I was off getting you this present!

Cresh hands Tubix a pile of rubbish.

Tubix: Uhhh . . . thank you?

Cresh: Where are you going?

Tubix: Uh? Nowhere! Nowhere at all, only strolling to uh . . .

Cresh: Well I should be leaving soon . . .

Tubix: Yes?

Cresh: Just to be away . . .

Tubix: I wouldn't desert my friends of course . . .

Cresh: Of course not! I should be leaving now.

Tubix: Of course, I as well . . . not to meet anyone, just to . . . walk. Thank you!

Cresh: Ciao!

They bolt off.

All But Tilly: Grumplestock?
Yes Grumplestock.
HERE!?
Now.
HERE!!!
More magic than anyone
LOOKING FOR HIS BABIES . . .
And now . . . left all alone . . .

A shift of energy as all but Tilly seep into the background, upstage. He is alone, now in the place of Suples.

Tilly: Hello? Hellooooo?

Hello?

Tubix . . . Morelle? Cresh even. No. I suppose I could have an imaginary friend.

Hello there? You look nice today. I look dirty? Well you're not much of a friend. I still like you though. Please! Don't leave! Well that's not very nice . . . goodbye then. Can't even keep imaginary friends . . . ohhhh how I'm blue . . .

Voices: Oh how I'm blue!

Tilly: Oh my.

Voices: Oh my.

Tilly: I guess I'm not alone here.

Voices: *Overlapping his speech.* I guess I'm not alone here.

Tilly: I don't see why you'd repeat me . . . my character's not incredibly stupendous . . . like Tubix perhaps. I've never had imaginary friends that have actually talked back. . . .

The three Suples approach from the darkness.

Suples: UUUUUUUUUP YOURRRRRRRS!

Tilly: Oh dear!

S1: Spare coin?

Tilly: Sorry.

S2: Drop a gold?

Tilly: None here.

S3: Help a man?

Tilly: I can't help myself.

Suples: Ahhhhhhh . . .

S1: Well that's no problem.

S2: Thanks there buddy.

S3: See ya later.

Pause. Tilly begins to leave.

Suples: Asshole.

Tilly: Hey!

Suples: Oh look!

S1: Spare coin?

Tilly: No.

S2: Drop a gold?

Tilly: Wha—

S3: Help a man?

Tilly: I told you!

S1: Hey stranger, I think I know you.

S2: Ahhhh shadup, ya don't know him. *To Tilly, indicating S1.* This guy's NUTS!

S3: You dinkers, he doesn't know us! Who are ya?

Tilly: My . . . name is Tilly.

Suples: *A welcoming cheer.* Whaaaaaa!

S1: Well welcome to the family!

S2: We'll treatcha okay!

S3: Even in this weather, ya know, all musty!

Tilly: Well . . . I only need to . . . I just need to become an important person . . .

Suples: Ahhhhhh . . .

Tilly: You can help me?

Suples: Hmmmmm . . .

S1: Well there's certainly different . . . uh—

S2: Levels . . . or levels . . .

S3: Of importance . . .

S1: I think—

S2: Maybe . . .

S1: I think—

S2: He thinks—

S1: I think—

S3: I think we'd better think . . .

The Suples think as Tilly watches nervously. They look back to him.

Tilly: Anything come up?

Suples: *Noticing him again as if for the first time.* Ahhhhhhh!

S1: Spare coin?

S2: Drop a gold?

S3: Help a man?

Tilly: I don't have anything, just like you.

Suples: OHHHHHHHH!

Tilly: May I ask why you're having trouble getting up?

S3: Ohhhhh well . . . it's how we're born, how we are, where we go, and what we'll always be. We CAN'T get up, because you see, well we would get up, I mean we could, because of the . . . except that . . . it's . . .

Tilly: Yes?

Suples: *Noticing him again as if for the first time.* Ohhhh!

S1: Spare coin?

S2: Drop a gold?

S3: Help a man?

Tilly: You can't get up. . . .

S3: Sorry.

S2: Sorry.

S1: Sorry.

S1: We can't get up.

S3: We can't get up because all of the Suples are already down, so if we try to help each other, there's no help in helping . . . only one of us could ever be up at once, and all of that drags the once holding up the hold down to the dirty ground.

Tilly: What holds you down?

Suples: The world.

Tilly: Will you ever get up?

S2: Only if the world helps us up.

S3: Which will never happen.

Tilly: Oh . . . that's sad . . . how do you live?

Suples: AHHHH!

S1: Spare coin?

S2: Drop a gold?

S3: Help a man?

Tilly: Oh.

S1: Try it. It's easy.

S2: *Extending a hand.* Just hold your arm out like this . . .

S3: And say the words . . .

Tilly stretches out his arm.

S1: Spare coin?

S2: Drop a gold?

S3: Help a man?

Tilly: . . . Money?

Suples: Ahhhhh!

Tilly: But . . . nobody is here. Nobody is walking by, how do you get anything?

S3: Well . . . we don't.

S2: But we have to do it.

S1: It's something to do.

Tilly: Don't your arms hurt after a while?

S3: No. Our arms have been stuck like this, outstretched, since our birth. No one loves us. And no one wants us.

Tilly: No one wants me either. My friends left without a word.

S2: Well you're lucky to even have friends!

S3: We're not even friends with each other . . . it's our nature.

Suples: OHHHHH!

We now shift to the brothel house.

Morelle: Mr. Stynhart! I'm so happy I arrived in time. The Glimmers. They come out at night—

Stynhart: Their dangers are common knowledge . . .

Morelle: Is it all right that I came back?

Stynhart: Certainly . . . what of your friends? Have you left them?

Morelle: Oh . . . I suppose I did . . .

Stynhart: How are you enjoying this fine, fair city?

Morelle: Well, today I . . . To tell the truth, Mr. Stynhart, this is the first city I've ever really seen. There's so much to take in. All the people and creatures and the market place—

Stynhart: There is no place quite like Bowble.

Morelle: Mr. Stynhart, you are so different from my father. You make me feel important.

Stynhart: Did your father reside near here?

Morelle: No. I shouldn't speak about him. *Pause.* Tell me more about what you do.

Stynhart: Your curiosity with—Morelle, this is a brothel house. I own Slips. I sell them to the men of Bowble. And, during the night, they please the rich and powerful, and they bring me money.

Morelle still does not understand.

Stynhart: The Knockentalks are celebrating their latest victory in gambling. I'm providing the entertainment.

Stynhart: Morelle, do you like to dance?

Morelle: Yes, of course. It's what I do.

Stynhart: Will you dance for me?

Morelle: Yes.

He plays as Morelle dances and begins to move more and more like a Slip.

Stynhart: Perfect.

A burst of laughter from the Knockentalks as we shift into the ballroom.

Fabious: Welcome to the Knockentalk ball, brothers! Avaunt ye, hehe, and let us begin the games!

K1: So, Fabious, are you looking for a new personal record tonight?

Fabious: As long as I keep the bets up, as usual, I think I'll be just fine.

K2: Well go on, I'm getting giddy, THROW IT!

Fabious tosses imaginary coin.

Fabious: There! Ten to one again, I have you.

K1: Again! AGAIN!

Fabious: What's the wager this time?

Tubix enters the room. He looks about curiously.

Fabious: Ahhh! Here for the ball I suppose?

Tubix: Uh—yes. I heard of it on the street.

K1: Knockentalks only!

Fabious: Oh shush up now! He's clearly one of us. Welcome, fellow Knockentalk. The ball is commencing shortly . . . any fee, entry, or gamble is permitted according to our recent coin gain.

K2: What will the bet be tonight?

K1: How many lights on the ceiling!

K2: Who will pass out first!

Fabious: Or how many Slips will arrive tonight!

Tubix: Slips!

K1: Oh, I can tell this man loves his Slips nice and slippery, don't you?

Tubix: Uh, well OF COURSE I do.

K2: I quite enjoy Stynhart's Slips . . . quite full tonight I hear.

Fabious: Excuse me gentlemen . . . *Clearing his throat loudly to the crowd.*

Feellooooow . . . KNOCKENTALKS! *A cheer.* I give to you our jewel of a queen . . . the governess of Bowble's centre . . . and the bringer of true happiness and prosperity to our kind . . . THE COUNTESS!

K1 becomes the countess.

Knockentalks: KNOCKENTALK SEPIK SOCK!
KNOCKENTALK SEPIK SOCK!
KNOCKENTALK SEPIK SOCK!

Countess: *Stern and direct.* QUIET! Stand aside Fabious. *He moves.* Fellow Knockentalks, Ten thousand coins were won last week in Tilroy by some very talented, well respected brothers of ours. The most anyone has ever earned in one evening. Excitement is absolutely rampant tonight, and the usual late night romp is in call as well. As the matriarch of our people, it is my duty to take time off of the governmental responsibilities, and to let loose . . . a little. Fellow Knockentalks . . . I'm sure now that we've raised the bar, there are plenty of Tilroy players ready to disarm you of that credit. Gentle Knockentalks, let's show Tilroy that we can up the ante and have Bowble celebrate Twenty thousand coins this week. *To Fabious.* LET US COMMENCE THE CELEBRATION FOR WHICH WE ARE SO DESERVING! KNOCKENTALK SEPIK SOCK!

Knockentalks: Knockentalk sepik sock, Knockentalk sepik sock, Knockentalk sepik sock!

The Knockentalks commence their game.

K1: I have a wager! Anyone need a wager? . . .

Fabious: Seven to six! Another wager? Anyone? . . .

K1: Fifty coins! Change for fifty coins!?

Fabious: How many buttons on his corduroy?

K2: Sepik Sock! I'll say five.

Fabious: Ten.

K1: Twenty.

K2: Twenty thousand!

All: Ahhhh!

Tubix: Uh—excuse me, but . . . I'm sorry, I've only just arrived and would like to start a wager . . . could you give me some advice?

K2: Of course, Sir Knockentalk. It's very important to be involved in this business.

Tubix: Important?

K2: Of course.

Fabious: Simple as nothing, sir. Simply make up your own game.

Tubix: Make up a game?

Fabious: Yes, a wager of your own. As they all do.

The game continues.

K1: Now . . . how many Slips will be naked tonight?

K2: All I hope!

Fabious: WAGER!

K2: Sepik Sock three.

K1: Four.

K2: Twenty.

K1: I'm done!

Fabious: No reply. Bantemo sepik sock!

He has won. Cheers.

K2: All right, what next!!??

Tubix: Uhhh—pardon, brothers?

Fabious: What's the wager?

K1: Wager it! Wager it!

K2: *Noticing the cufflinks on Tubix' shirt.* CUFFLINKS!

K1: GRAND!

Fabious: ARE THEY EXPENSIVE?!

Tubix: Yes. They're foreign.

K1: FOREIGN!

K2: Oooooo!

K1: Ah! Were they handmade?

Tubix: *Partly aside.* Yes, actually . . .

Fabious: How long have you had them?

Tubix: Well, since I was—

K1: Have they had any other owner?

Tubix: I've had them my whole . . . life.

K2: LET'S WAGER THEM!

Tubix: Wager?

All: YES!

Fabious: What's your game of choice?

Tubix: I don't really have a game of—

K1: How many guests have arrived!?

Fabious: How many letters in your last name?

Tubix: I don't have a last—

K2: Who will have at the most Slips tonight?

K1: How many creases are in the walls?

K2: How many times the countess will visit the restroom?

Fabious: We did that last time!

All: Ahahaha.

K1: SO, tell us. What is your game?

Tubix: *Struggling.* How about a game of . . . Definition. I'll give you a word and you define it. If you can't define it—

All: Then we lose.

Fabious: Got it!

K1: Let's play!

Tubix: All right then. Machionio!

Fabious: Machionio. That isn't a word.

Tubix: Oh yes it is.

Fabious: No it isn't. Use it in a sentence.

Tubix: Ah, but that would have me winning the game for you. Would it not?

K1: Machionio. The weather is machionio tonight.

Tubix: Incorrect. Next.

K2: Machionio. A greeting. Machionio!

Tubix: Wrong.

Fabious: I want some machionio.

Tubix: Incorrect. Incorrect. Machionio. Definition: The source of which a spindling steno pipe links up with the lactated telenosis existor noun at the finale of a curtain. Such as: Machionio.

All: *Different degrees of trust and excitement. Cheer. They hand him money.*

Tubix: Shall we have another?

Stynhart's violin cuts the sound of the ball. All at attention.

Tubix: What's that music? It's wonderful.

K2: That's Cartsmen's violin. The Slips are ready for us!

Fabious: I can't wait . . . I've been itching all night!

Tubix: What for?

K2: Raw meat my friend. The fresh, sweet meat of Slips.

Tubix: The Slips . . .

K1 has become a Slip. Fabious and K2 bring it toward Tubix.

Others: KNOCKENTALK SEPIK SOCK!
KNOCKENTALK SEPIK SOCK!
KNOCKENTALK SEPIK SOCK

The Slip is put in front of Tubix. Pause.

Tubix: Is this a new game???

A shift. Cresh scampers off into the darkness to meet Grittle.

Cresh: And the juice of this flower shall be your doorway to fame and importance . . . and you shall play as a child does . . . without fret, or fear . . . but out of folly and fun. And one day . . . you shall see that THIS is what you were meant to do . . . where is that man . . . that dark Grittle . . . this is where he said to meet. . . .

Grittle appears.

Grittle: Good evening Cresh.

Cresh: Grittle . . . a wonderful evening, no?

Grittle: The streets of Bowble are fettered with fears.

Cresh: But not for Cresh.

Grittle: Yes . . . I can see that.

Cresh: So . . . why did you call me here? What am I to do? What is important?

Grittle: Well Cresh, I'm sad to say that even in the sinful heart of this city, there are amongst us those who possess morals. It makes my line of work difficult.

Cresh: But, I play the game well, no?

Grittle: Yes, Cresh. You act on instinct. Oh your energy, your power. You've already proven to be something unique.

Cresh: Well, it comes as no surprise . . . I am my own self.

Grittle: I suppose so.

Cresh: So . . . how would you make use of my purpose?

Grittle: A joke! I need you to put something in a man's eye.

Cresh: Dehahaha! A joke, eh?

Grittle: Yes. And you know of the flower that you took?

Cresh: Yes. Was fun.

Grittle: Well. The juices of this flower are what I want you to give to his eyes, Cresh.

Cresh: Ahahahah!

Grittle: Yes? Is that funny?

Cresh: Very! Yes, aahahhaha! So why would you play a joke on that man? Cartsmen Stynhart.

Grittle: Take the flower's nectar Cresh. And give it to his eyes. And you can come and do pranks, and steal, and play with us as much as you'd like.

Cresh: AAHHHHHHH! Wonderful! And I thought I had no friends in Bowble!

Grittle: You thought wrong, my friend. Well Cresh . . . you'll play this trick . . . tomorrow. In the meantime . . . we must take rest. The Glimmers approach.

Cresh: Yes . . . it's getting darker.

A shift to Suple territory. Tilly with the three Suples.

Tilly: It's getting darker.

S2: Yes.

S1: Another evening of pain.

Tilly: What?

S3: And every night, the Glimmers come out.

S2: Oh yes.

S1: I almost forgot . . . why did you remind me?

Tilly: The Glimmers! Oh no . . . can't we hide? They'll hurt us.

S2: It makes no difference to us. They only hurt to the verge of dying . . .

S1: I see them coming.

Tilly: Oh no.

S2: They never kill. They leave us out always. Suffering forever.

S1: I see them!

Tilly: Oh no!

The Glimmers' music plays, as the three Suples become Glimmers, attacking Tilly.

Tilly: Oh . . . no! No! Help! Help me! It hurts! Ohhh!

A shift . . . we follow Tubix and the Knockentalks on the street.

Knockentalks: Knockentalk sepik sock, make a bet, it's one to get, Bantemo sepik sock knockentalk! Aha!

Tubix: Why did we leave the ball?

K2: The Glimmers are parting . . . now's the time to clean up the night's scraps old chum!

Fabious: Well, Stynhart's Slips only go a certain distance anyways.

K2: When you've had your fun, there are other endeavors out in Bowble!

Fabious: The Suples are out of course. Left behind by the Glimmers.

Tubix: Suples? I know of them.

Fabious: Of course . . . you know the Suples . . . the scum of the city, the tainted spots on our existence . . . those ones.

K2: Ahahaha!

Fabious: And it's always a tradition upon celebration, or—well any night for that matter.

K2: Tradition to proceed into the streets for the Knockentalk romp!

Tubix: Sounds absolutely delightful! How do you wager this one?

Fabious: Oh, hardly a wager!

K2: Hardly!

Fabious: Since the Glimmers have already been out, there'll be filthy Suples everywhere! It's always fun to give a little nightly bashing after good Slips!

Tubix: Ahhh! Aha, excellent!

Fabious: Just hang around friend, and you'll see just how EXCELLENT things can REALLY be!

They find Tilly, hurt and moaning.

Tilly: Ughhh . . .

K2: Lookit THIS one! Ugly as ever!

Tubix: Tilly . . .

Fabious: Ohhoho!!! Fresh Suple for the beating!

Tilly: What's going on?

The Knockentalks laugh, exchanging glances.

K2: Always speaking nonsense!

Tubix: Filthy scum!

Tilly: Who said that?

Tubix: Uh—I, Tubix, the newest Knockentalk council member . . . quiet, vermin!

K2: Very good!

Fabious: Well done! Shall we continue with the classic Bantemo version of torture!

Tubix: Uh—YES, we shall! Pray, may I ask what that is?

Fabious: Oh, you'll see when the wonderful, spectacular show comes!

Tilly: TUBIX! It's you! Tubix?

K2: *To Tubix.* Do you know him?

Tubix: Queer Suple . . . always talking nonsense! Come . . . Bantemo!

A shift. The four address the audience.

All: Grumplestock is here.
Yes?
He's closer now.
YES?
Looking for his children?

Cresh with Grittle, Morelle with Stynhart.

Cresh: Now it's the time? Time now yeah?

Grittle: Yes. It's time to play the game . . .

Cresh: YES!

Grittle: Clear your mind . . . focus only on his eyes.

Cresh: And when he is too close, the trap will be sprung.

Grittle: You will have him

Cresh: He will be mine?

Grittle: You will win the game . . .

Cresh: Hehe . . .

A shift of light. On the stage opposite of Cresh and Grittle, a scene with Morelle and Stynhart.

Stynhart: Morelle, you must stay.

Morelle: But, Mr. Stynhart—

Stynhart: You are too important to let slip away.

Morelle: I am important?

Stynhart: Of course, my dear.

Morelle: But my friends . . .

Stynhart: Forget your friends!

Shift back to Cresh and Grittle.

Grittle: Do not speak or breathe. . . .

Cresh: Yes . . . strike quickly.

Grittle: Very good . . . and next.

Cresh: Next I grab him.

Grittle: Very good.

Cresh: And surprise him, hurt him, silence him!

Grittle: . . . very good.

Cresh: And win the game!

Grittle: FORGET THE GAME, CRESH, do you understand my HATE for this man?! You must remember your purpose . . . this is the most important job I've ever given. . . .

Back to Morelle and Stynhart.

Stynhart: Stay with me, Morelle. I only want to play for you. Don't you want to dance for me?

Morelle: Yes.

Stynhart: Don't you love me, Morelle?

Morelle: Yes.

Stynhart: Then stay with me, Morelle.

Morelle: Yes.

She kisses him.

Stynhart: Perfect.

Stynhart leaves her. The boundaries of the locations are broken. Cresh's eyes follow Stynhart.

Cresh: All right . . .

Morelle: I love him—

Cresh: I hate him—
  Now is the time.

Morelle: Love . . .

Cresh: Hate.

Morelle: Important.

Cresh: I'm important.

Cresh/Morelle: Important.

In a mysterious shift, Cresh finds Stynhart. Their eyes meet. Unexpectedly, Cresh murders him. A shift. We follow Tubix, Tilly, and the other Knockentalks, taking Tilly to be killed and chanting "Bantemo."

Fabious: Ready sirs? Shall we commence the ceremony?

K2: Are you ready to burn, Suple scum?

Tilly: Why do you keep calling me that?

Tubix: Uh—because that's the filth that you are! Suple!

Tilly: Tubix?! Can't you see it's me? It's TILLY! One of
  Grumplestock's.

Fabious: Suples are always talking such nonsense. *Dragging
  him up to a stake.*

K2: *To Tubix.* Come now, help us.

Tubix: This will be great fun.

Tilly: It's TILLY!!! Can't you see?

Tubix: And can't you SEE that I am a Knockentalk! Suples
  don't speak that way to us.

They force him to an imaginary stake.

Fabious: Commence the cleansing! Bring the fire forth!

Tubix: *Perking.* Fire?

K2: Fire B-R-R-Rought— *laugh* dahahah . . .

Tilly: F-i-i-i-ire?

Tubix: Fire?

Fabious: Exciting, is it not? Bantemo, Bantemo—come now . . .

Fabious/K2: Bantemo . . . Mano Bantemo. Basseke! Mano Bantemo Bassekel! Knockentalk, Knockentalk, Knockentalk!

Fabious: BURN HIM!

Tilly: Ohhh no!

Tubix: FIRE! FIRE!

Tilly: NO!

Tubix: STOP!

Tubix douses the fire before any damage is done.

Fabious: What is your problem?!

Tubix: You'll hurt him doing that!

K2: That's the point!

Fabious: What are you doing?

Tubix: I am . . . I am helping a friend. I'm helping Tilly, fellow marionette of Grumplestock's.

Fabious: You filthy traitor.

K2: Leave him with his little pet Suple then.

Fabious: Well . . . we thought you were of some noble blood . . . you can forget any kind of importance you may have had with us . . . farewell.

The Knockentalks leave.

Tubix: Tilly, I'm—

Tilly: You hurt me.

Tubix: Did the fire catch you?

Tilly: No . . . the fire doesn't matter Tubix. I've never felt before . . . so sad . . . so . . .

Tubix: Please, don't tell me . . . just come along. . . .

Tilly runs off. We shift to the brothel house. As Morelle enters, she discovers Stynhart dead on the floor.

Morelle: Mr. Stynhart? Hello? Mr. Stynhart!

She finds the flower. She seems happy at what she thinks is a present. Two Slips emerge from upstage.

S1: Hello, dear.

S2: We've seen you coming in.

S1: A friend of his, I take it.

S2: Yes.

S1: But now . . .

S2: Your man is dead.

Morelle: What?

S1/S2: Dead.

S2: Cartsmen is dead.

Morelle: Dead?!

S1: Sad?

S2: Grieved are you? You don't know grief! You can't understand our happiness to this man's death.

They gradually approach closer.

S1: Imagine . . . since our birth—

S2: Strutted about this city of sin—

S1: Toys for the rich—

S2: And relief for the filthy—

S1: Hit, tortured, beaten, slapped—

S2: Raped as many times as time would allow—

S1: Over and over.

S2: COMPLETE

S1: FULL

S2: UTTER

S1/S2: SORROW! Completely aware of the terrors inside us every day! No rest . . . no relief . . . .no soul . . . screaming on the inside, and panting on the outside . . .

S1: You can't feel what we've felt . . .

S2: But now that he's dead . . .

S1: You can come close . . . close to what we've felt . . .

S2: But if you grieve for him . . . you deserve no better than Cartsmen himself . . .

S1/S2: It's your turn. . . .

They take her. We have a change of scenes. We see Tubix walking with a weak Tilly.

Tubix: I'm sorry Tilly.

Tilly: Unhhh . . .

Tubix: I don't know what was going through my head.

Morelle stumbles away from her place, and meets Cresh.

Morelle: Cresh . . .

Cresh: Morelle?

Cresh: You found my flower!

Tilly: Why were you hurting me?

Tubix: I was . . . I was with those people . . . they were so much like me, so sophisticated. . . .

Morelle: *Realizing what has happened.* . . . You . . . killed Stynhart.

Cresh: Stynhart? I played a trick on him.

Morelle: You killed Mr. Stynhart!

Tilly: I thought you were my friend, but I was wrong . . .

Tubix: NO Tilly, please, I stopped them, I stopped it. They were awful, awful people, and YOU are my friend.

Tilly: How did it feel Tubix? How was it to feel so proud?

Cresh: I'm sorry.

Tubix: Well . . . how was it to feel so alone . . .

Cresh: I'm sorry.

Tilly: It was the most pain I've ever felt. . . .

Cresh: Morelle . . . what was it like to love?

A shift. They address the audience.

Tilly: That was the last of the city that I remember. . . .

Cresh: We are getting closer now.

Morelle: Somewhere in the centre of the city, near some dark buildings—

Tilly: Something inside us was saying that our paths were closing in—

Cresh: And it wasn't us that had explored Bowble—

Tubix: It was Bowble that had explored us.

A shift as Gramaphone Lady comes forth.

Grama: Tonight is the night that it will finally happen. Tonight is the night I have foreseen. And what was meant to come has not happened. You four have deceived yourselves . . . to become important is to find your own belonging . . . to become as belonging with those you belong with as you can. You did not try to listen. You did not attempt to see. The city stands strong in its place . . . I TOLD YOU!! And you let the temptations of your silly faces be swallowed, eaten by the guile and misfortune of this fortress.

The story's pages continue to turn. But my foresight cannot span as far as you've gone. Remember my words, because now it seems you are in a new light.

Full moon. Midnight. Exactly where we are. You four deserve any deserving which deserves your company. May fate and life bring you back to your minds. The future is clouded and uncertain. BUT one thing I do see . . . your time in Bowble is at an end.

Voices: Grumplestock?
Yes Grumplestock.
Here?
Here.
Now?
NOW!

Tilly: The idea of him coming BACK . . . was like a dream. . . .

Cresh: Father Grumplestock was here . . . father Grumplestock had lost us . . . Grumplestock's children had done wrong in a wherabouts in which they didn't belong . . . Grumplestock rounded a Bowble street and found them . . . Grumplestock began to speak. . .

All: And GRUMPLESTOCK . . . was FURIOUS!

Grumplestock: FOUND at last! Puppets of magic descent, bow now, and feel the world's gravity. YOU HAVE BROKEN YOUR MAGIC! YOU EXIST TO ME NOW BUT AS FRAGMENTS OF A FAILED WORK!

Too curious for your own box, You have been born . . . you have lived a life not meant for you . . . and so, with the box open, you must now complete a cycle and learn of death . . . another part of life locked to yourselves. . . .

The light from the beginning of the play hits them, dim and mysterious.

Tilly/Cresh	**Tubix/Morelle**
Too many feelings	No Space
All at once	No light
This is the horror	Only magic
This is the consequence	
Of being human	

All: NOTHING LEFT!!!
  No no
  No no
  No no
  NO . . . NO . . .
  LET . . . US . . . LIVE!!!

A pause as they reach towards the light. They break, and address the audience.

Tubix: Did you like our story . . . ? Please say you liked our story.

Cresh: It's the only one of our own which we've had . . .

Morelle: And only the first time we've told it.

Tilly: I must admit . . . it feels sad, now that it's finished.

Tubix: Yes . . .

All: Finished.

They pause. Then speak to each other.

Tubix: Back in the box we sit.

Tilly: Where we've been trapped for as long as we can remember . . .

Cresh: No space.

Morelle: No feeling.

Tubix: No room.

Tilly: No light, but for a shred.

Morelle: It's better than out there. . . .

Cresh: Curse him . . . curse our father!

Tubix: Cresh, THIS is where we belong.

Cresh: But now that we know Bowble—

Tubix: And the hurt we caused each other . . .

Morelle: And ourselves.

Cresh: But to be trapped in here is like . . . it's like—

Tilly: It's a full moon tonight.

Tilly's comment 'brings them back'.

Morelle: Find your purpose. Find what you are.

Tubix: Discover your importance.

Cresh: Are we not all but masks?

Tubix: We are but faces . . .

Tilly: Wood and paint.

All: We are Grumplestock's.

Morelle: And we are important.

Cresh: But our adventures and experiences in Bowble . . .

Tubix: Have changed us somehow . . .

Tilly: Those are the memories we hold now.

Morelle: There is a way and a flow to everything . . .

Tilly: The darkness of humanity . . .

Tubix: The blackness of the earth and this box that holds us . . .

Cresh: But we want to have more.

Tubix: To know more.

Morelle: To feel more.

Tilly: To BE more.

Cresh: To find . . . and live . . . and create . . . MORE STORIES.

Morelle: Because now we have our OWN story.

Cresh: A story we've lived.

Tilly: And felt.

Tubix: And just finished telling you.

All: Together.

Morelle: As we belong.

Pause.

All: Thank you.

END

Marie (Colleen Feehan) and Susan (Clarice Eckford) eat grapefruit
while Richard (Stephen Kent) sleeps in *Citrus*.

Citrus
a play in two acts, eight scenes

Janis Craft

Citrus first came to my attention in the lobby of the Roxy Theatre shortly after the submission deadline for 2004. I had set up my script reading shop on a long table with a number of piles of paper. When I picked up *Citrus*, the most obvious and tallest of the piles was the "NRY" (not read yet) pile.

When I'm making my first pass through script submissions I try to put myself imaginatively in the mind of the audience. I want to know if the script can live on stage. I want to know if the script has personality and soul. In the first read, the technical aspects of writing don't interest me as much as a good story told with passion. *Citrus* was such a story for me. Usually, I read a play, make my notes and move on to the next one from the "NRY" stack. With *Citrus* I read it again—a guilty pleasure because I had so many plays that I hadn't even read once. I took it into the theatre and read it there. I stared at the stage and imagined what it could look like. I e-mailed the playwright and asked her a dozen questions. I imagined what choices I would make if I were to direct it, whom I would cast, what palette I would employ, etc. I imagined what it would be like to act in the show myself. I wondered about the background of the characters, the music they listened to, the books they read, the painters they admired. I wondered what happened to them after the play was finished. I found myself caring about them and being frustrated by their limitations. Suffice it to say, it grabbed me.

Because Janis was in Chicago during rehearsals, communication between the playwright and the production team faced a significant hurdle. To help bridge this gap, Janis created a blog where everyone involved had the opportunity to dump their thoughts, images, and experiences. While the ideal is to have the playwright in the rehearsal hall, the blog experience was an excellent second-best solution.

Citrus is a juicy play and is governed by the irrational. Set in an exotic (and erotic) locale and playing on its themes of taboo, it should have the effect of making both actor and audience alike feel a little dizzy when it's done. The Nextfest production was a bit marred by the fact that I underestimated the running time of the show when putting together the big picture schedule. As a consequence, the actors had to pick up the pace. While this is a practice I generally favour, here it tended to work against the hypnotic rhythm of a sultry languid Mediterranean dream. When the playwright arrived in Edmonton to see the show, she was surprised at how many laughs the audience offered. She described the effect as "darkly comic."

Here is how Janis wrote about the play in the program for "The Citrus Project" later in 2004:

> I wasn't sure why I was writing *Citrus* when I first began except that I had this image that wouldn't leave me of two women sitting on a beach, one of whom was wearing a large, black hat and no top. So I waited, I watched, I listened, and I dreamt until Richard, Marie, and Susan developed from that image and started commanding me to look at the world through their eyes. This is what I've begun to see: People don't touch each other enough. If they did, if they put down their personal lenses long enough to feed each other grapefruit or invite each other into their dreams or if they just touched two non-sexual parts of their bodies together, they would understand that intimacy can be as simple as feeling another human being's blood rush under your skin, on the other side of your skin, so that you forget what is inside and what is outside. What is you and what is both of you. Where you stop and they begin. Intimacy is letting go and making yourself vulnerable to the possibility that you may be changed. You may get lost. You may go entirely through someone else and come out somewhere you've never been only to find yourself alone again.

While the script calls for two hotel rooms, Melissa Cuerrier's design for the Nextfest production presented one room that served as both. Set dressing showed whether we were in the newlyweds room or not. It was mostly done through pillows. Lots and lots of pillows. The bed was built on a rake to facilitate visibility (the Roxy stage is elevated above most of the audience). Hanging drapes moved in the wind of electric fans—which were onstage and operated by the actors—ostensibly to keep their characters cool in the hot Spanish night which was backlit by a cyclorama saturated with colour.

– S.P.

PRODUCTION HISTORY

Citrus received a staged reading in May of 2003 at Theatre School of DePaul University directed by Joshua Saletnik and featuring Leslie Kies as Susan; Steve Haggard as Richard; Elisabeth Ford as Marie. In June of 2003, the dream scene from *Citrus* was read as part of the Literary Managers and Dramaturgs of the Americas Conference. The scene was directed by dramaturg Gavin Witt. In January of 2004, New Theater Collective (Chicago) put together an informal reading of the play (from which came the decision to produce it).

The Nextfest 2004 production was presented at the Roxy Theatre with the following team:

Susan: *Clarice Eckford*
Richard: *Stephen Kent*
Marie: *Colleen Feehan*
Director: *Elizabeth Day*
Stage Manager: *Skye Perry*
Designer: *Melissa Cuerrier*

New Theater Collective had another reading of *Citrus*, which featured Katie Jeep as Marie; Lindsay Morton as Susan; Braden Moran as Richard. September 9–October 11 2004, New Theater Collective's production of *Citrus* ran at the Springman Studio in Chicago as part of "The Citrus Project", a multimedia event featuring *Citrus*, a *Citrus*-inspired art exhibit, and guest performances by local musicians, dancers, and performance artists following the show each night.

Susan: *Katie Jeep*
Richard: *Eric Slater*
Marie: *Kelli Nonnemacher*
Director: *Elisabeth Ford*
Stage Manager: *Mary Ellen Rieck*
Costumes: *Jason Loper*

Music: *Steve Haggard*
Producer: *Kelly Hoogenakker*

THE CHARACTERS

One man, Two women—all late '20s / early '30s

Richard: Twin brother to Susan, newlywed to Marie.
Susan: Twin sister to Richard.
Marie: Newlywed to Richard.

THE SETTING

A hotel and nearby beach somewhere in Spain. The scenes all take place on the beach, in Richard and Marie's hotel room, or in Susan's hotel room.

SYNOPSIS

When newlyweds Marie and Richard travel to the beaches of Spain to meet with Richard's twin sister, Susan, the last leg of their European honeymoon suddenly takes on a surprising new flavour. Susan, who has always been more than close to her twin, finds herself for the first time competing for his affection. Marie, fascinated by Susan's uninhibited and aggressive nature, begins to crave her sister-in-law's attention more than her new husband's. Richard, trying to salvage his quickly dissolving marriage, is forced to confront his inherent attraction to his twin. Caught between desire and necessity; intimacy and identity; dreams and reality, each one struggles to stay afloat in a quickly rising, citrus-flavoured sea.

Citrus

ACT ONE
SCENE ONE

A remote, mountainous beach in Spain. Marie and Susan are sunbathing. Susan has on a large sun hat and no top.

Marie: One thing?

Susan: One odd little thing.

Marie: His hands.

Susan: Ah hah.

Marie: They're always so warm.

Susan: And you like it when he runs them all over you.

Marie: He gives good back rubs.

Susan: Like he's kneading dough.

Marie: Yeah.

Susan: Steady. Strong. Never too fast.

Marie: Sometimes too hard.

Susan: That's when it gets good.

Marie: I'm kind of sensitive.

Susan: He said. What does he like you to do?

Marie: He doesn't like his back rubbed. He says it—

Susan: *Interrupting*—tickles? You're not doing it hard enough. *Beat.* When we were little he used to like me to walk on him in high heels.

Marie: What?

Susan: He'd lie on his back and have me walk on his stomach and chest. Sometimes I'd jump.

Marie: He liked this?

Susan: Loved it. He'd beg me to.

Marie: He asks me to bite him sometimes.

Susan: Where?

Marie: The crook of his shoulder.

Susan: Right here?

Marie nods.

Marie: I don't think I do it right.

Susan: Do it harder.

Marie: I don't want to draw blood.

Susan: You won't.

Marie: It's funny to be talking about this.

Susan: With me, you mean.

Marie: I don't talk to anyone about these things.

Susan: You should. How else do you expect to get tips?

Marie: I used to read Cosmo. Vanity Fair. I guess their tips are all the same.

Susan: But this isn't, is it?

Marie: Nope. Not exactly.

Susan: Consider it my wedding present.

Beat.

Marie: You must feel like you know things about him, I mean, sense things—unspoken things—because you're his twin.

Susan: I don't FEEL like it, I do. I know him better than he knows himself.

Marie: That's hard to imagine.

Susan: Give me your hand.

Marie: Why?

Susan takes Marie's hand and puts the inside of her wrist to the inside of Marie's.

Susan: Can you feel my pulse?

Marie: Uh . . .

Susan: Just wait a minute.

Marie closes her eyes. A minute.

Marie: I'm not sure if it's yours or mine.

Susan: That's what it's like.

Marie: That's incredible.

Susan: Even when we're not touching.

Marie: Do you think it's from hearing each other's heartbeat before you were born?

Susan: It's more than that.

Marie: *Pulls her hand away.* I know you mean a lot to him. He was really glad you could meet us here.

Susan: We always said we'd get to Spain.

A moment.

Marie: When I was little, I used to wish that I had siblings. I thought my parents were awful for not giving me one. You're lucky to be a twin.

Susan: I am. *Beat.* Didn't you ever have a friend you were really close to? A best friend?

Marie: Sure. I had a few.

Susan: Are you still friends?

Marie: Not with them . . . no.

Susan: What happened?

Marie: Um. I don't know. They moved? We changed?

Susan: It must have been hard losing them.

Marie: It was part of growing up.

Susan: Maybe.

Marie: I did have this one really close friend . . . Jessie. . . .

Susan: A girl?

Marie: Jessie? Yes.

Susan: What happened?

Marie: We got in a fight over Barbie dolls or something and then she made new friends. I remember being really lonely when we stopped playing together.

Susan: How old were you?

Marie: Six? Seven?

Susan: Did you ever kiss?

Marie: Kiss?

Susan: Kiss.

Marie: That's a strange question.

Susan: Why? Kids do that.

Marie: Yeah . . .

Susan: Didn't you?

Marie: Um . . . I guess we tried it. . . .

Susan: I always wondered what it would be like to have girl friends. If it would have been the same.

Marie: Kissing?

Susan: Playing.

Marie: Oh. *Beat.* Did you and Richard . . .

Susan: Did we what?

Marie: Never mind.

Susan: Never mind?

Marie: Sorry.

Susan: That's what Richard likes about you.

Marie: What?

Susan: This. The . . . never mind. The blushing. I'm sure he thinks it's cute.

Marie: I'm not sure that's what I'd call it.

Susan: What would you call it?

Marie: Annoying.

Susan: Is it?

Marie: Sometimes it'd be nice to say what's in my head and not worry what it sounds like. Remove the filter and just . . . let go. Like you.

Susan: Then do it. What do you want to say?

Marie: I don't know.

Susan: What's in your head?

Marie: *Shaking her head.* Un-uh.

Susan: You just have to do it and not care.

Marie: That's easier said than done.

Susan: Exactly. So just say something. Anything. Don't think.

Marie: Um . . .

Susan: First thing that pops into your head.

Marie: Okay . . . um . . .

Susan: Go!

Marie: *Laughs. Takes a deep breath.* You have nice breasts.

Susan: Good! And thanks.

Marie: Not that I was looking but they're . . .

Susan: Say it.

Marie: . . . hard to miss. *They laugh.*

Susan: Great. I like yours too.

Marie: They're small.

Susan: They're average. Say something else.

Beat.

Marie: Uh. . . .

Susan: Come on. Say something outrageous.

Marie: I'm not thinking anything outrageous.

Susan: Liar.

Marie: I'm not.

Susan: Then teach me how to kiss a girl. I've never kissed one. Can you believe it?

Marie: Um . . . No . . . ?

Susan: Come on. It'll be funny. You can pretend I'm Jessie.

Marie: I was a kid. It's not like I—

Susan: It is annoying. Don't you want to let go?

Marie: I . . . *Beat.* I guess I don't.

Susan: *Putting on her top.* Well, at least now you know.

Marie: Yeah . . .

Susan: It's important.

Marie: What is?

Susan: To know. Where you stop and someone else begins. Especially if you're going to let go. *Packing up her bag.* We're doing dinner at nine?

Marie: Yeah . . .

Susan: *She puts her hat on Marie.* Here. You're gonna fry.

Marie: Where are you going?

Susan: To look for Richard.

Marie: He's out shooting.

Susan: I'll find him. Adios! *She starts to walk away.*

Marie: Susan?

Susan: Hmm?

Marie: Nothing. Sorry.

Beat.

Susan: It's okay. *Susan comes back and kisses both of Marie's cheeks.* It really is cute. So's the hat. You should keep it.

Susan exits. Marie watches her and then she takes off the hat, examines it, and decides to put it back on.

SCENE TWO

That evening. Richard and Marie enter their room.

Marie: You're bad doing that in front of her.

Richard: We were just playing.

Marie: I know.

Richard: Wait. Just like that.

Richard gets his camera.

Marie: Richard.

Richard: It's perfect.

Marie: Don't you have enough of me yet?

Richard: I'll never have enough. Your head. It was almost touching the door.

Marie: Like this?

Richard: Uh huh . . . And your mouth was open. You were saying something. What was it?

Marie: I don't remember . . .

He snaps the picture.

Richard: There. That's going to be a good one.

Marie: *Kissing him.* They're always good.

Richard: No . . . There's something about you tonight.

Marie: Sangria? *She flings off her shoes.*

Richard: There is. *He takes another picture.*

Marie: Richard . . .

Richard: I can't help it . . . you're just so . . . so . . .

Marie: Come here.

He goes to her. She puts his camera down and wraps her arms around him.

Richard: . . . .ravissante. You're ravissante.

Marie: French?

Richard: *Nods.* Ravishing.

Marie: Oh right.

Richard: You're bella et . . . *He licks her nose.* . . . dolci.

Marie: Italian . . .

Richard: And . . . what was that German one?

Marie: Reizvoll.

Richard: Danka. But most of all . . . Te voy comer.

Marie: Hot. Where'd you learn that one?

Richard: Suze.

Marie: Really.

Richard: She wasn't going to tell me at first. Said she didn't know if it was appropriate for a honeymoon. I had to buy her a beer to get it out of her.

Marie: What does it mean?

Richard: Are you sure you want to know? *Marie tries a sexy face.* Okay. It doesn't really translate but literally it means: I'm going to eat you. Te voy comer.

Marie: I don't know if I should be excited or frightened.

Richard: Both. *He licks her skin.* Mmm. You taste . . .

Marie: Sweaty?

Richard: Un-uh.

Marie: I should. I was lying out there forever.

Richard: Tangy.

Marie: Tangy? Like spicy?

Richard: No . . . almost sweet, but not. It's good. Faint. But good. *Richard licks Marie.*

Marie: Richard.

Richard: What?

Marie: The phrase isn't literal.

Richard: I know. *He kisses her passionately. She pulls away.*

Marie: You taste like cigarettes.

Richard: Thanks.

Marie: Well you do.

Richard: I had one of Susan's.

Marie: Since when do you smoke?

Richard: Not since high school. But Suze started again and . . . I really wanted one today.

Marie: It's fine. I was just . . . What did you two do earlier?

Richard: We had a beer. Caught up. She taught me dirty Spanish phrases to make you hot.

Marie: You talk about that sort of stuff?

Richard: We talk about everything. That doesn't bother you . . . ?

Marie: No . . .

Beat.

Richard: I'm not starting or anything.

Marie: It's fine.

Richard: I can brush my teeth.

Marie: Really. It's—

Richard: Te voy comer?

She smiles. He goes to kiss her and grabs her face.

Marie: Don't!

Richard: What?

Marie: Sunburn.

Richard: Oh. Right.

Marie: It's sensitive.

Richard: I'm sorry.

Marie: It's okay.

Richard: We should put some aloe on it.

Marie: It'll be fine.

Richard: It'll hurt worse tomorrow if you don't.

Marie: It'll be okay.

Richard: I'm telling you—

Marie: Richard, I don't want any aloe.

Richard: Please? I want to rub it on you.

Marie: Oh, there's the truth. *She sighs.* What scent is it?

Richard: I'll go check. *He gets it in a hurry.* Coconut?

Marie: Fine.

Richard: Thank you.

Marie: Be gentle.

Richard: Of course. *He slathers her with aloe massaging as he goes.* Not bad, huh?

Marie: No. Not bad. Except for the smell.

Richard: I kind of like it.

Marie: You would.

Richard: When we were little Suze used to eat this shit.

Marie: What?

Richard: Coconut lotion and cherry chapstick. You'd think we didn't feed her.

Marie: That's disgusting.

Richard: I know. *He gets a little carried away with the aloe.*

Marie: Those aren't burnt.

Richard: So I can't touch them?

Marie: Massage.

Richard: But I love your breasts.

Marie: Shut up.

Richard: I do.

Marie: They're small.

Richard: They're ripe and juicy and I want to eat them.

Marie: They're small and I'm getting ready for bed. *She starts getting ready for bed.*

Richard: Ouch.

Marie: You're too drunk, anyway.

Richard: I'M too drunk?

Marie: You were talking about cherry chapstick.

Richard: I haven't been drunk since . . . .

Marie: Since our wedding night?

Richard: Yes. Our wedding night.

Marie: You were too drunk.

Richard: Thank you. I'd forgotten.

Marie: Sorry, but you had that coming.

Richard: Love you too.

Marie: You did.

A beat. Marie stares in the mirror Richard watches her.

Marie: Maybe I'll get implants.

Richard: Could you ruin the mood a little more?

Marie: Susan's are perfect.

Richard: Apparently you can. *Beat.* Have you been staring at my sister's tits?

Marie: It's kind of hard not to when she's sunbathing topless.

Richard: She's always showing them off. The slut.

Marie: I would too if I were her.

Richard: No you wouldn't. You won't even let me touch them.

Marie: If I were her.

Richard: You're not.

Marie: Obviously.

A beat.

Richard: What's going on with you tonight?

Marie: Nothing. I'm getting ready for bed.

Richard: Well then stop staring at your tits and hurry up. You're killing me.

Marie: Am I?

Richard: You are.

Marie: Am I 'killing you softly'?

Richard: And you're accusing ME of being drunk?

Marie: You'd better watch out.

Richard: Oh yeah?

Marie: Yeah . . .

Richard: Come and get me.

Marie: You don't know what you're in for . . .

Richard: I don't?

Marie: I'm feeling naughty tonight.

Richard: How naughty?

Marie: I think I might put on my heels naughty . . .

Richard: And then what?

Marie: You know what.

Richard: I do?

Marie: You do.

Richard: Just get over here. I can't take it any longer.

Marie lurches herself onto him and bites his neck.

Richard: Ow!

Richard grabs his neck and laughs.

Marie: What?

Richard: I love you.

Marie: Did I do it too hard?

Richard: You're adorable.

Marie: Why are you laughing?

Richard: Because you're adorable and I love you for it. Come here.

Marie: Adorable?

Richard: Yes. You're adorable. Now let me kiss you.

Marie: Fuck you.

Richard: What?

Marie: Goodnight. *She rolls over.*

Richard*: Confused.* What?

Marie: Good. Night.

Richard *Unbelieving.* Goodnight?

Marie: Yes.

Richard: You're kidding.

Marie: Take a picture of this. *She flicks him off.*

Richard: Marie. Come on.

Marie: *Emphatically.* Good night.

Richard lies there for a few minutes waiting for her to turn to him but she doesn't. He tosses and turns and all she does is pull the covers tighter. Finally he gets up. Marie doesn't budge. He dresses. She feigns sleeping. He grabs his camera and leaves the room.

SCENE THREE

Richard stands outside Susan's hotel room and finally knocks on her door. She opens it wearing her nightgown. He takes her photo. She smiles and lets him into her room.

Susan: Bad dream?

Richard: Something like that.

Susan: I can't sleep either. It's too hot.

Richard: No shit.

Susan: Want a beer?

Richard: Where'd you get beer?

Susan: I found a store down the beach a ways.

Richard: Oh.

Susan: Do you want one?

Richard: Are they cold?

Susan: Probably not.

Richard: All right.

She gets two beers. Hands him one and they sit down.

Susan: *Holding up her beer.* Salud.

Richard: *Sounding it out.* Sa-lud?

Susan: *Nodding.* Salud.

Susan clinks bottles with him. They drink.

Susan: I take it Marie's asleep.

Richard: Too much sangria.

Susan: Passed out?

Richard: Right in the middle.

Susan: That's nice.

Richard: Now that you mention it . . .

Susan: Shut up.

Richard: Oh?

Susan: It's been a little dry over here.

Richard: You've got the nightgown on.

Susan: It's hot.

Richard: You didn't meet anyone on your walk?

Susan: Nope.

Richard: That's too bad.

Susan: I'll survive.

Richard: Me too.

Susan: Until morning, you bastard.

Richard: Yeah. Well. That's the perk.

Susan: The perk?

Richard: Why not.

Susan: She told me she bites you.

Richard: What else did she tell you?

Susan: That she likes my breasts.

Richard: No she didn't.

Susan: She did.

Richard: Shut up.

Susan: She wanted to touch them.

Richard: You're terrible. Now I'll really have fucked up dreams.

Susan: I know.

They laugh. A beat.

Richard: I saw you two out there.

Susan: I bet we made a good picture.

Richard: I got a few nice shots.

Susan: Good composition?

Richard: Yes, good composition. *Beat.* What were you talking about?

Susan: Oh you know . . . you.

Richard: Wonderful.

Susan: What else do we have to talk about?

Richard: You said you'd be nice to her.

Susan: I was.

Richard: Uh huh . . .

Susan: I was. For you.

A moment. Suddenly Richard points to her strap, which has fallen from her shoulder.

Susan: What?

Richard: Your strap . . . *He reaches over and fixes the strap. He lingers touching her a moment.*

Susan: Do you remember . . .

Richard: . . . when I came home from school and you were swimming laps. In your prom dress.

Susan: That's not what I was going to say.

Richard: Well, I do remember that.

Susan: What I was GOING to say was—

Richard: —-when *Grease Two* was your favourite movie?

Susan: Not it.

Richard: At least laugh.

Susan: When we were thirteen and—

Richard puts up his finger to stop her. He concentrates for a minute. Susan smiles.

Susan: —go ahead.

Richard: —and Dad took us sailing. Out on the Chesapeake.

Susan: And I got seasick. And we had to go back early.

Richard: Yeah. I remember.

Susan: You were really mad at me, weren't you?

Richard: I got over it.

Susan: You stopped telling me your dreams after that.

Richard: It wasn't because you got sick.

Susan: Then what was it?

Richard: I don't know . . . I stopped caring about you making my bed?

Susan: Hey. That was a nice trade-off. It kept you from getting in trouble.

Richard: I guess I did get the good end of the deal.

Susan: It was fair. I didn't mind making your bed. And I loved hearing your dreams.

Richard: I didn't believe you for the longest time.

Susan: That I didn't have them?

Richard: I thought you were just making it up so I'd tell you mine. But you said once that I must have taken them from you before we were born. Somehow that made sense to me.

Susan: I said that?

Richard: Yeah. And I felt guilty so I'd try really hard to remember. I thought they were somehow half yours.

Susan: Maybe they were.

Richard: You were in most of them. *Beat.* My favourite ones were about us flying.

Susan: Yeah. Mine too.

Richard: I remember it felt like swimming.

Susan: Through really thick liquid.

Richard: And it felt like if we concentrated hard enough . . .

Susan: . . .we'd actually start . . .

Richard and Susan: Floating . . .

A moment. They both concentrate.

Richard: It never worked.

Susan: No . . .

Richard: You didn't concentrate hard enough.

Susan: That's what you'd always say.

Richard: You didn't.

Susan: I tried to.

Richard: Well. It's not like it was possible anyhow.

Susan: You were always so pessimistic.

Richard: Realistic.

Susan: Same thing.

Richard: One of us had to be.

Richard finishes his beer and kisses her on the head, about to leave. Susan grabs his hand suddenly.

Susan: *Suddenly.* Lie down with me.

Richard: What?

Susan: I want to try it again. I want you to tell me a dream.

Richard: I don't have them anymore.

Susan: Don't tell me that.

Richard: I don't.

Susan: Then tell me an old one.

Richard: I don't remember them.

Susan: Yes you do. You remember the flying ones.

Richard: I remember THAT we were flying.

Susan: Then make something up. I don't care. Just lie down and start talking. I want to close my eyes and remember.

Richard: Suze.

Susan: What?

Richard: I have to go back.

Susan: I know. It'll only take ten minutes.

Richard: I shouldn't.

Susan: I gave you a beer, didn't I?

Richard: And I drank it.

Susan: You want another?

Richard: I can't fall asleep here.

Susan: I know. Just stay until I do. One more beer.

A beat.

Richard: One more beer.

Susan gets Richard another beer. Susan turns down the lights and lies down, putting her head in his lap.

Susan: Comfy?

Richard: I guess.

Susan: Then what are you waiting for?

Richard: I've got to think of one. Do you have any requests?

Susan: Make me believe it.

Richard: Right. So . . . *He closes his eyes and thinks for a while.* Okay. So there's this house, big house . . . on the water. Lots of windows. One side is all windows. And it looks out onto this huge dock with all of these boats—maybe five or six. A couple of speedboats, a sailboat, a rowboat. Some Jet Skis. And they're all . . . ours.

Susan: Nice.

Richard: Yeah. No parents.

Susan: How old are we?

Richard: I don't know yet.

Susan: But we live together?

Richard: We don't live together. But the boats belong to both of us. And you're coming over to use one . . . yeah, there you are.

Susan: What am I wearing?

Richard: A bathing suit.

Susan: That's all?

Richard: And your hair is in those braids.

Susan: So it's long?

Richard: Do you want me to tell this or not?

Susan: I'm just trying to picture it.

Richard: It's long. You come inside through one of the big glass doors and you go to the kitchen. You're pouring yourself an iced tea when I come down. I get a beer, but you tell me that I should have some of the iced tea because it's really good. Then we decide to take one of the Jet Skis out together. We pick this high-tech one that's so light I can just pick it up and put it in the water. It's like a balloon. We get on and—

Susan: Can I drive?

Richard: No you can't drive. It's my dream.

Susan: Please?

Susan bats her eyes. Richard sighs.

Richard: So you decide that you want to steer and I get on the back and we're driving away from the dock. My feet are dangling in the water and it's really warm. Really, really, warm. Like bath-water warm. A big boat goes by and you turn off the engine so we can rock in the wake. And you're still drinking this iced tea. Telling me how good it is. I don't know how you got it out there, but you did.

Susan: *Half asleep.* I'm smart . . .

Susan yawns and nestles into him more. Richard strokes her hair. Susan closes her eyes.

Richard: *Quietly.* And suddenly I'm really thirsty. You give me a sip. And you were right, the iced tea is really good. Very sweet. And while I'm drinking it, a big wave bumps me off into the water. It's so warm. And I'm feeling almost drunk from the tea, but I've still got the glass in my hand. I can't seem to let go of it and it's heavy and I'm sinking. *Beat.* Are you asleep?

She doesn't answer. He lies down with his face next to hers and breathes in her breath.

Richard: But I don't mind because it's so pretty under the water . . . and warm. It feels like I'm floating, but it's heavier . . . much heavier. And I don't know which way is up anymore. *He strokes her face.* And I don't care.

Richard curls in to Susan and closes his eyes. Susan opens her eyes. Lights out.

SCENE FOUR

A few hours later, a knock on the door. Susan wakes up with

*Richard's arm around her. She doesn't want to get up but she
answers the door. Richard is still asleep.*

Marie: Hi. Sorry to wake you up but have you seen Richard?

Susan: Yeah. He's sleeping.

Marie: Here?

Susan: I gave him two beers and he passed out.

Marie: Oh.

Susan: I guess I did too. *She yawns and stretches. A beat.* Did
   you want to come in?

Marie: Yeah.

*She comes into the room. She stands quietly looking at Richard.
Susan looks at her.*

Marie: Well. He's asleep.

Susan: Yep. *She starts digging through her bags.*

Marie: *Awkward.* I didn't know where he was.

Susan: *Still searching.* Right here. Asleep.

Marie: He should have told me where he was going.

Susan: He didn't want to wake you up.

Marie: I wasn't sleeping.

Susan: Oh.

*Susan finds what she's been looking for: a grapefruit. She begins
peeling it. Marie watches her for a moment.*

Marie: Is that a grapefruit?

Susan: It is.

Marie: You peel a grapefruit?

Susan: How else would I eat it?

Marie: Cut in half. With a spoon.

Susan: And sugar?

Marie: So it's not so bitter.

Susan: It's not bitter.

Marie: Right.

Susan: It's good.

A moment.

Marie: So.

Susan: Yeah?

Marie: This is kind of an odd honeymoon.

Susan: How so?

Marie: Well. My husband and I got into an argument last night and now—

Susan: An argument?

Marie: He didn't tell you?

Susan: He just said . . . He didn't make a big of a deal out of it.

Marie: It wasn't.

Susan: What?

Marie: A big deal. At least it wasn't last night.

Susan: And this morning?

Marie: Well. He's here.

Susan: He is.

Marie: In your bed.

Susan: Asleep.

Marie: And I don't really know what to think about that.

Susan: You don't like me very much, do you?

Marie: I like you.

Susan: I make you uncomfortable.

Marie: No . . . it's just . . . This. This makes me uncomfortable.

Susan: THIS being . . . ?

Marie: Your relationship.

Susan: We're twins.

Marie: And you're very . . . close . . .

Susan: And that makes you very . . . jealous?

Marie: No. I'm just . . . I'm just . . . I don't know. I never had a brother and certainly not a twin but somehow I just don't think this—

Susan: But now you have a sister.

Marie: You?

Susan: And so do I. I've never had a sister before.

Marie: Yes. I guess we are . . . sisters-in-law. . . .

Susan: So stop worrying. We'll get used to each other.

Marie: Right.

Susan pulls the membrane away from a segment. She bites into it, slurping. Marie watches her curiously. When Susan notices Marie's fascination, she laughs.

Susan: Would you like some?

Marie: What?

Susan: You're staring.

Marie: Oh. Sorry.

Susan: I can tell you want to try it.

Marie: No . . . I just . . . I've never seen . . .

Susan: Here. You'll like it.

Susan tears off another membrane and hands Marie a piece of grapefruit. Marie takes a bite.

Susan: Good, isn't it?

Marie: So good.

Susan: Told you.

Marie: *Licking her fingers.* I'm a mess.

Susan: That's the best part.

Marie: I've never had anything so good. . . .

Susan: *Suggestively.* You don't say . . .

Marie: Can I have another piece?

Susan: *Laughs. Starts to give Marie another piece, but stops.* Isn't Richard satisfying you?

Marie: Why?

Susan: I'm teasing. You seem pretty . . . hungry.

Marie: Oh. Well. I guess I am.

Susan: *Slurping on the piece of grapefruit tauntingly.* So then he's not.

Marie: No, actually. I guess he's not.

Susan: Really.

Susan hands Marie another piece who takes it greedily.

Marie: He slept here last night.

Susan: So you didn't . . .

Marie: I thought he told you this?

Susan: I like hearing your side.

Marie: My side . . . *Beat.* I guess I was kind of terrible about it. He wanted to, but I wouldn't . . . On our honeymoon.

Susan: Why wouldn't you?

Marie: I don't know. The whole thing was pretty ridiculous. I just don't like how he sees me sometimes . . . He makes me feel so . . . boring.

Susan: I don't think you're boring.

Marie: Well that's . . . something.

A beat. Susan hands Marie a new, whole grapefruit.

Marie: Oh. Um . . . thanks . . .

Maire tries to peel the grapefruit isn't sure where to start.

Susan: Just dig into it and rip off the skin.

Marie begins peeling.

Susan: Keep peeling.

Marie has peeled all of the outside skin off.

Marie: I peel this too?

Susan: Until there's nothing left but the inside. Good.

Marie begins peeling the membranes and slurping the fruit.

Marie: Mmm . . . I swear this is the best . . . God . . . I can't believe I never . . . damn . . .

Marie peels and devours the grapefruit with increasing excitement and abandon until there is only one small piece of it left. She looks to Susan holding it guiltily.

Marie: I'm sorry . . . I . . .

Susan opens her mouth and closes her eyes. A beat. Marie puts the fruit into Susan's mouth. Suddenly Susan bites Marie's finger.

Marie: Ow!

Susan: Didn't draw blood, did I?

Susan lets Marie hang for a beat before she finally laughs. Marie laughs with her hesitantly.

Marie: I can't believe you bit me.

Susan: How was it?

Marie: How was what?

Susan: The grapefruit.

Marie: Oh. Well . . . My hands are sticky.

Susan: *Laughs, hands her a towel.* I bet.

Susan picks up Richard's camera. She looks through the lens at Marie, but doesn't take a picture. Instead she snaps a close-up of Richard's sleeping face and then sits back on the bed next to him. She gets comfy.

Marie: Did you two used to sleep together?

Susan: Well . . .

Marie: *Dryly.* When you were little.

Susan: Sure we did.

Marie: Often?

Susan: He was afraid of the windows in his room. So he slept with me.

Marie: Why was he afraid of them?

Susan: They were huge and bare.

Marie: Why didn't your parents put up some blinds?

Susan: Why didn't yours tell you not to kiss girls?

Marie: They didn't know.

Susan: There you go.

Beat.

Marie: Jessie and I never KISS-kissed.

Susan: Uh huh.

Marie: Did you and Richard?

Susan: What if we did?

A short moment and then Marie decidedly stands, walks to other side of the bed and lies down next to Richard.

Susan: What are you doing?

Marie: Lying down.

Susan: This is my bed.

Marie: Don't you want to see what he'll do?

Susan: I know what he'll do.

Richard moans and then rolls toward Susan, putting his arm around her. Susan giggles.

Richard: *Very groggy, eyes still closed.* What's so funny?

After a moment, he opens his eyes and sees Susan. He senses another body and turns over to see Marie who closes her eyes just in time. He turns back to Susan.

Richard: *Whispering.* What the fuck?

Susan: Uh. Morning.

Richard: *Whispering.* What are you doing here?

Susan: This is my room.

Richard: *Still whispering.* Why is she . . . ?

Marie: *To Richard.* Kiss me.

Richard: Marie. You're awake . . .

Marie: Kiss me.

Richard: What?

Marie: Kiss me.

Richard: Now?

Marie: Why is it such a big deal?

Richard: It's not, it's just . . .

Marie: I want you to kiss me.

Richard: Why?

Marie: You're my husband.

Richard hesitates and then leans over to kiss her quickly but she pulls him and presses her mouth to his. He tries to match her kiss but she pulls away.

Marie: *To Susan.* Did it feel like that?

Susan: Did what?

Marie: Kissing.

Richard: Kissing who? What's going on?

Susan: How would I know? *She lights a cigarette.*

Marie: She knows.

Susan: I don't.

Richard: Would someone please—

Marie: Ask her.

Richard: Susan?

Susan: I don't know what she's talking about.

Richard: Marie?

Marie: Yes she does. Ask her.

Richard: Suze? Please tell me what's going on.

Susan: I would if I knew. This was your wife's idea.

Richard: Marie?

Marie: Hmmm?

Richard: What was your idea?

Marie: This was not my idea.

Richard: Oh my God. One of you? Please?

Marie: *To Susan.* Can I have a cigarette?

Susan looks at her amused, then to Richard. She shrugs and starts to get a cigarette.

Richard: Marie.

Marie: What?

Richard: I'm not awake

Marie: You're awake.

Susan looks at both of them still holding the cigarette. Marie takes the cigarette out of Susan's hand.

Richard: I can't be.

Marie: *To Susan.* Thanks. *She begins to exit.*

Richard: Where are you going?

Marie: Talk to your twin.

Marie exits. Richard looks to Susan.

Susan: You married her.

Richard: This is some nightmare, right? It has to be.

Richard shakes himself awake. A beat.

Richard: What the fuck did you tell her? *Grabbing her.* What did you tell her!

Susan: Calm down.

Richard: What!

Susan: Hey! Concentrate. *She takes his face, steadies him a second.* What would I tell her?

Richard stares at her hard and then exits, slamming the door.

Susan: What would I tell her.

Susan puts out her cigarette and flops back onto the bed. She notices Richard's camera. Lights out.

ACT TWO

SCENE ONE

Marie and Richard's hotel room. Richard is pacing. Marie enters wrapped in a towel. Her hair is wet.

Richard: Marie. Where have you been?

Marie: I went for a swim.

Marie goes to change. Richard follows.

Richard: I've been looking for you everywhere.

Marie: Sorry.

Richard: What the hell happened earlier?

Marie: When?

Beat.

Richard: You're naked.

Marie: I am.

Richard: Where's your bathing suit?

Marie: I didn't wear one.

Richard: What?

Marie: You heard me.

Richard: You didn't wear one?

Marie: I didn't want to.

Richard: In public? Marie.

Marie: What? It's okay if Susan does it, but not me?

Richard: Susan . . . *Beat* What happened this morning?

Marie: You mean when I found you sleeping in her bed?

Richard: I fell asleep there.

Marie: You did.

Richard: She didn't tell you that?

Marie: She did.

Richard: So then what happened?

Marie: When?

Richard: This morning, Marie.

Marie: You were asleep.

Richard: Yes. And why did I wake up in her bed with you next to me!

Marie: I should be the one yelling. *Beat.*

Richard: I'm sorry. I'm confused. Everything's just so . . . upside-down.

Marie: I know.

Richard holds her.

Richard: Maybe we should go back to bed. It's late and we're not making any sense.

Marie pulls away from him.

Marie: It's morning, Richard.

Richard: It was an idea.

Marie begins packing her suitcase.

Richard: What are you doing?

Marie: I'm not going to sleep with you anymore.

Richard: What?

Marie: I'm not going to sleep with you.

Richard: You're not going to sleep with me right now or you're not going to sleep with me tonight?

Marie: Right now. Tonight. Maybe every night.

Richard: You're kidding.

Marie: No. I'm not.

Richard: Marie. This is our honeymoon.

Marie: It doesn't really feel like one does it?

Richard: No, it doesn't. Not since you started being weird last night.

Marie: Since I started being weird?

Richard: You roll over without even a kiss good night and now you don't want to sleep with me? On our honeymoon? That's weird.

Marie: It's because you can't sleep with me, Richard.

Richard: Last night I couldn't. Because we had a fight.

Marie: You never can.

Richard: Of course I can. I've been sleeping with you for months now.

Marie: But you're not comfortable.

Richard: Comfortable? I'm comfortable.

Marie: You toss and turn. You don't sleep, not really.

Richard: I'm fucking comfortable.

Marie: You keep me awake.

Richard: I keep you awake?

Marie: Yes. And I'm tired.

Richard: That's what this is about?

Marie: Do you think I slept at all last night?

Richard: I'm sorry but I couldn't lay there next to you like that. And the heat. I was so fucking hot. What was I supposed to do?

Marie: I'm tired of thinking about you. About you being comfortable. You sleeping.

Richard: Marie.

Marie: So I'm not going to anymore.

Richard: Marie, tell me what this is about.

Marie: I just told you.

Richard: No you didn't.

Beat.

Marie: Do you like kissing her better?

Richard: *Incredulous.* Who? Susan?

Marie: I know. When you were little. It's okay.

Richard: You think we've kissed?

Marie: I know things. I'm not ignorant.

Richard: What do you think you know?

Marie: That you've kissed. That she used to walk on you in high heels. That you like sleeping with her better than you do with me.

Richard: Did Susan tell you this?

Marie: She didn't have to.

Richard: It's not true. She's my sister, Marie.

Marie: So? I got in that bed with both of you because I wanted to know what it was like to feel you sleeping and I felt more than that.

Richard: Listen, I don't know what you're thinking but this is my sister we're talking about. My twin sister.

Marie: Can you really tell yourself that everything is normal with her?

Richard: Yes!

Marie: Richard.

Richard: Yes.

Beat.

Marie: What if I kissed her?

Richard: What if?

Marie: Yesterday. On the beach.

Richard: You didn't kiss Susan.

Marie: What if I did? What if I wanted to feel what you felt?

Richard: What if? Did you kiss my sister?

Marie: It'd be like kissing you, wouldn't it?

Richard: Did you?

Marie: We were intimate.

Richard: So then you didn't.

Marie: Intimate is more than you and I are.

Richard: Right now that's for sure.

Marie: We've never been.

Richard: Right . . .

Marie: We haven't.

Richard: So let me get this straight. We've been married three weeks and you were intimate, but not with me. With my sister. Intimate but you didn't kiss. Well. I guess that was the idea. Meet her here so you guys could get to know each other. Get fucking intimate. What the hell does intimate mean?

Marie: Give me your wrist.

Richard: Tell me Marie.

Marie: Give me your wrist. *She takes his wrist and puts it to hers.* Can you feel my pulse?

Richard: Tell me.

Marie: Can you? *He pulls his arm away.*

Richard: No!

Marie: I can't feel yours either. But I felt hers and I couldn't tell which was mine.

Richard: Is that it? Is that what was intimate?

Marie: She said she doesn't know where you stop and she begins. Do you feel that way too?

Richard: She was fucking with you Marie.

Marie: Do you?

Richard: She was fucking with you! That's what she does.

Marie: It doesn't matter. I felt it. And I felt it again this morning when you were asleep.

Richard: You're not making any sense.

Marie: I'm just telling you what I felt.

Richard: I wish you wouldn't.

Marie: I'm sick of pretending, Richard.

Richard: So then stop it and say something that makes sense.

Marie: We've both been pretending.

Richard: We have?

Marie: This whole honeymoon. Even Paris.

Richard: Right.

Marie: I'm glad I got to see all of those places but we've been going to these cities and then to museums or castles, eating at restaurants and having sex and the whole time we're smiling for your pictures, pretending like this is all that we could possibly want even though you can't sleep at night and I run out of things to say at dinner and every time we have sex we're trying to make up for the wedding night which we can't even talk about. *Beat.* The thing is, I know they'll be great pictures. We'll look happy in them. Blissful even. I think it's become a habit for us.

Richard: You realized all of this this morning?

Marie: I've known it. We both have.

Richard: No. Not me. I actually was happy.

Beat.

Marie: I wasn't unhappy . . . I just . . .

Richard: What?

Marie: Susan said that she knows you better than you know yourself and I don't feel like I know you at all.

Richard: You know me.

Marie: I don't. I don't even know if you wanted to get married or if you just did it because it seemed like you should because it was time.

Richard: Of course I wanted to.

Marie: I don't know.

Richard: Marie.

Marie: I don't.

Richard: I shouldn't have asked her meet us here.

Marie: No.

Richard: I'm sorry. Things weren't supposed to go like this.

Marie: But they did.

Richard: And I'm sorry. I've said that. I'll keep saying it. What else do you want?

Marie: Everything. I want you to miss me like you've missed her. I want to eat grapefruit until my mouth bleeds. I want to walk out of here right now and not know what's next except that I'll never go back to being so . . . satisfied.

Richard: And I'm supposed to just sit in this hotel room with my fingers crossed hoping that my wife will decide to come back sometime soon?

Marie: No. You should figure out what it is that you want.

Richard: I know what I want. I want my wife, who I married because I thought she was rational, to stop with this crazy bullshit and I want my life to go back to normal. I want to finish this honeymoon and then I want to go back and pretend like it never happened.

Marie: That's romantic.

Richard: Well?

Marie: Well I want more.

Richard: Maybe you should have thought about that before we got married.

Marie: Maybe.

Marie gathers her bags.

Richard: I can't believe this.

Marie: Your life was never normal, Richard.

Richard: Did Susan tell you that too?

Marie: And I don't think that's at all what you want.

Marie takes her bags and exits. Richard notices one of the many grapefruit that have begun to accumulate between scenes. He throws it.

SCENE TWO

Susan's room. Susan is still in bed. There is knocking on her door. Susan tries to ignore it and stay asleep. The knocking continues and she finally opens the door. Marie is standing there holding Susan's hat.

Marie: You were sleeping?

Susan: Trying to. I take it you weren't.

Marie: No. I wasn't.

Pause. Susan waits for Marie to say more.

Marie: Here. I came to give this back to you.

Marie hands the hat to Susan.

Susan: Okay.

Marie: I thought you'd want it.

Susan: I do. Thanks.

Marie: Okay. Well. See you.

Marie begins to leave.

Susan: What were you doing? While I was trying to sleep.

Marie: Oh. Swimming. I went for a swim.

Susan: Refreshing?

Marie: Yes, it was. It helped me sort some things out.

Susan: What did you come up with?

Marie: A lot of stuff. *Beat.* I realized that I don't enjoy kissing Richard.

Susan: That's quite a realization.

Marie: It was. *Beat.* What do you think love tastes like?

Susan: I didn't know it had a taste.

Marie: I used to think it tasted sweet. And thick, like chocolate. But I was wrong. It's saltier. I think it must taste like the ocean.

Susan: And what does Richard taste like?

Marie: I don't know anymore. But I don't think I like it.

Susan: That sounds like a problem.

Marie: Yeah.

Beat.

Susan: What did you really come to say?

Marie: I don't know.

Susan: Yes you do.

Beat.

Marie: Are you in love with him?

Susan: No Marie. I'm in love with you.

Marie: Are you?

Susan: He's my twin. I love him dearly.

Marie: It doesn't matter if he's your twin. Are you in love with him? When you think of him do you taste the ocean?

Susan: Um . . . No.

Marie: Please, just answer me.

Susan: Why?

Marie: Because I felt it. Between you. And I just want to hear you say that it's real. That I'm not crazy for leaving.

Susan: You're leaving?

Marie: Yes.

Susan: When?

Marie: My bags are already downstairs.

Susan: Does he know?

Marie: I packed them in front of him.

Susan: You're leaving and he knows.

Marie: This is what you wanted, isn't it?

Susan: What?

Marie: For me to go.

Susan: It's your honeymoon.

Marie: And it's your dream to be here with him.

Susan: Sure. Here we are.

Marie: With me right in the middle.

Susan: You're not in the middle.

Marie: Right.

Susan: What did you tell him?

Marie: I told him that I wasn't going to sleep with him anymore. That I was sick of pretending we were comfortable together. I told him to figure out what it is that he wants.

Susan: He doesn't know what he wants?

Marie: He won't admit it.

Susan: Maybe that's because there isn't anything to admit. Maybe he has everything he wants.

Marie: He wants things. He wants them desperately but he won't go for them, not really. He's not like you in that way.

Susan: What way?

Marie: You want what you want and you go for it even if it seems completely impossible. You don't let anything, anyone, get in your way.

Susan: That's not true.

Marie: You say whatever's on your mind. You're uninhibited.

Susan: You don't know me very well.

Marie: It's not a bad thing. It's honest. I admire you for it.

Susan: You shouldn't.

Marie: I do. You made me feel what it's like to want something, to really want it, and now I see all of the things there are to want.

Beat.

Susan: He loves you.

Marie: I'm not sure.

Susan: It's in his pictures of you.

Marie: It's in his pictures of you.

Susan: You can love more than one person.

Marie: Maybe.

Susan: You love them differently.

Marie: I don't want to be loved differently.

Susan: That's not what I meant. I—

Marie: I should go.

Susan: You can't leave him.

Marie: Why not?

Susan: He won't know what to do with himself.

Marie: You'll help him figure it out.

Susan: It should be the other way around.

Marie: But it's not.

Beat.

Susan: You can't leave.

Marie: I'm not going to lie next to him another night and act like everything's okay.

Susan: You don't have to stay with him. You can stay with me.

Marie: With you?

Susan: Yeah. Stay with me.

Marie: What's the point of that?

Susan: We're sisters.

Marie: Not if I leave him.

Susan: Then we're friends.

Marie: You think we're friends?

Susan: Why not? It'd be a first for me.

Marie: Having a friend?

Susan: A girl friend.

Marie: You've never been friends with a girl?

Susan: I haven't.

Marie: I don't believe you.

Susan: Girls didn't like me.

Marie: Why not?

Susan: They liked Richard. But I didn't like them either so it worked out.

Beat.

Marie: I like you.

Susan: Thanks.

Marie: I do. And better than I like Richard right now.

Susan: Then stay.

Marie: I can't.

Susan: Please?

A beat. Marie takes Susan's face in her hands and kisses Susan gently on the lips in an honest moment of intimacy and friendship.

Marie: Goodbye.

Marie starts to leave.

Susan: You can't leave him.

Marie: Why?

Susan: Because I won't know what to do.

A vulnerable moment. Susan attempts to light a cigarette but can't get it lit. Marie takes the cigarette and lights it. She sits and they share the cigarette.

Richard enters.

A full moment.

Marie passes the cigarette back to Susan and she puts it out quickly.

Richard: *To Marie.* Why are you here?

Susan: I'll leave you two.

Richard: *To Susan.* Tell me what you told her.

Marie: I shouldn't be here.

Marie starts to leave.

Richard: *To Susan.* Tell me.

Susan: *To Marie.* Marie, what did I tell you?

Marie: *To Susan and then to Richard.* I'm sorry.

Marie exits.

Susan: I never told her anything.

Richard stares at the door.

Richard: I don't know what to do.

Susan: Richard.

Richard: *Starting to cry.* I don't know what to do . . .

Richard reaches for Susan. She wraps her arms around him. A real brother/sister moment. The moment lasts too long. They become aware of it. It's awkward for them. The awkwardness grows. They pull away from each other suddenly. It hits them. All of it. Susan turns away.

Richard: I'll go . . .

Richard leaves. Susan doesn't stop him.

Susan sits. She looks around. She packs her things then sits down to write a letter as . . .

. . . Marie goes to the beach and sits on her luggage and Richard gets drunk on tequila.

SCENE THREE

Susan enters Richard's room carrying his camera. He's drunk and playing with one of the many grapefruits on the floor.

Susan: *Noticing the grapefruit.* What are you doing?

Richard: Getting intimate.

Susan: I was afraid you'd be drunk.

Richard: *Holding two grapefruit to his chest.* Touch them. I know you want to.

Susan: You shouldn't have been alone.

Susan takes the grapefruit from him and hands him his camera then begins cleaning up the grapefruit around the room.

Richard: Why do you have my camera?

Susan: You left it in my room. *He looks at her through the lense.*

Richard: How do you like it?

Susan: I only took one picture.

Richard: No. How do you like kissing Marie? *He takes a picture of her.*

Susan: You talked to her?

Richard: She talked to me.

Susan: When? Just now?

Richard: This morning.

Susan: She said that this morning?

Richard: She said everything this morning.

Susan: So you haven't seen her . . .

Richard: What does she taste like? Does she taste like me?

Susan: How many shots have you done?

Richard: I'm not doing shots.

Richard drinks from the bottle. Susan tries to take the bottle out of his hand.

Richard: Hey.

Susan: You're going to puke.

Richard: I don't puke.

Susan: Yes you do. Senior prom? Tequila's not your friend. *She takes the bottle from him.*

Richard: Senior prom. Amy Venza. I forgot about that. Was she a lesbian too?

Susan: Lie down, Richard. You're going to fall over.

Richard: Was she? She wouldn't put out, I remember that.

Susan: She wouldn't put out because you threw up on her pink satin dress.

Richard: Pink satin. I don't remember that. Why do you remember that?

Susan: Because I wasn't trashed.

Richard: Why not?

Susan: Because I had to take care of you. Now lie down.

Richard: You went home with her, didn't you? That's why she wouldn't put out. She liked you. She was a lesbo.

Susan: I went home with you that night, Richard.

Richard: How come? 'Cause you're a lesbo?

Susan: Because someone had to get you into the house before Dad found you.

Richard: Lesbo . . .

Susan: Will you drink some water?

Richard: Water . . .

Susan: Good.

Susan goes to get the water.

Richard: Suze?

Susan: Just a minute. *She comes back with the water.* Now drink.

He drinks.

Richard: Suze?

Susan: More.

He drinks more.

Richard: How long you been a lesbo?

Susan: Richard, I didn't kiss Marie. Now lie down.

He lies down with his head on her lap. She strokes his head.

Richard: She said you did. Or what if you did. I don't know what she said.

Susan: She probably said a lot of things. She was confused.

Richard: I think we made her confused.

Susan: I think everyone's confused.

Richard: Why did I marry her?

Susan: Because you love her.

Richard: Do I?

Susan: Yes.

Beat.

Richard: How come you don't have boyfriends?

Susan: Richard, I'm not gay.

Richard: I know. But how come?

Susan: I don't like anybody.

Richard: Nobody?

Susan: Not in the morning.

Richard: Don't you think that's weird?

Susan: It's just how it is. No more questions, okay?

Beat.

Richard: She knows. She has to know. I was so drunk.

Susan: Come on. Lie down. *Susan gets him to lie down.*

Richard: Four whisky sours on an empty stomach. And then just whiskey. Straight.

Susan: You were drinking tequila.

Richard: Not at the wedding.

Susan: No. Not at the wedding. *Beat.* I drank whiskey too.

Richard: I was so nervous and she knew. It's a big deal signing away your life. I had cold feet.

Susan: Of course you did.

Richard: Freezing feet. And they didn't go away. Afterwards I should have been able to enjoy the prize. She wanted it. She was hungry for me. I could taste it when she kissed me.

Richard laughs.

Susan: You're funny.

Richard: But it wasn't funny. It made me dizzy. Sick. Ughh . . . nauseous.

Susan: Don't talk about it.

Richard: The thought of filling her up right then . . . ughh . . .

He leans over to throw up.

Susan: There you go. *She strokes his head.*

Richard: She knew it wasn't the alcohol. She knew.

Susan: It's okay. You'll feel better now.

Richard: I couldn't do it and she knew why.

Susan: Shhh. Relax.

Richard: Do you know why?

Susan: Go to sleep, Richard. Please. Just sleep. *He lies quietly with his head on her lap.*

Richard: Suze?

Susan: No more questions, remember?

Richard: Tell me a dream.

Susan: I don't have them.

Richard: Yes you do.

Susan: No, that's your job.

Richard: How come?

Susan: Because it always was.

Richard: I'll finish my dream.

Susan: And then will you go to sleep?

Richard: Yes.

Susan: Promise?

Richard: Promise.

Susan: Okay.

Richard: Where'd I leave off?

Susan: You were underwater. With the cup.

Richard: That's right. And it's warm. It's warm under the water, Suze. You should get in.

Susan: I'm in.

Richard: You are?

Susan: I'm in.

Richard: Okay. You're under the water with me. Isn't it warm?

Susan: It's warm.

Richard: I like being under the water with you. It's like when we were little. In the pool. Remember?

Susan: Uh huh.

Richard: Except we're not kissing. We used to kiss, didn't we? Under the water? That's what you told Marie.

Susan: I didn't tell her that.

Richard: We did. I remember. In the deep end. Under the diving board. How come under the diving board? So no one could see?

Susan: We didn't kiss.

Richard: Not for a long time. When was the last time?

Susan: We didn't kiss.

Richard: You don't remember?

Susan: Because we didn't.

Richard: I remember.

Susan: Maybe you dreamt it.

Richard: Did I?

Susan: You must have.

Richard: That day I told you about Marie. You were in the pool.

Susan: We didn't kiss then.

Richard: Maybe I wanted to.

Susan: But we didn't.

Richard: No. We didn't. Not then. How come?

Susan: Because we didn't. Now go to sleep.

Richard: Suze?

Susan: Go to sleep, Richard.

Richard: What if we kissed now?

Susan: We wouldn't.

Richard: But what if we did?

Susan: I'm leaving, Richard. That's what I came to tell you. *She takes a note out of her pocket and lays it on the bed. She's almost in tears.* I wanted to get you to sleep but I can't wait any longer.

Richard: No.

Susan: I have to.

Richard: Please don't.

Susan: You know I have to.

A moment. Richard tries to kiss Susan. She stops him. She starts to leave.

Susan: I'm going.

Richard: You shouldn't have asked me to stay last night. You knew I'd sink.

Susan stops in the doorway.

Susan: I did have a dream once. I must have forgotten it because it scared me so much. *Pause.* I dreamt I was drowning and it was so real. *Pause.* Goodbye Richard.

Susan exits. Richard stares at the door for a long time. Finally he picks up the note.

SCENE FOUR

Marie sits on the beach next to her suitcases obsessively picking away at several grapefruit. She's made quite a mess. Richard walks up behind her. He watches her for a while. Finally, he goes to her.

Richard: So. Is your mouth bleeding yet?

Marie: What?

Richard: Earlier. You said you wanted to . . . She left.

Marie: Oh.

Richard: *Holding the note.* Paris, apparently. *Sitting next to her.* I would've told her it's overrated. *Pause.* That's a lot of grapefruit.

Marie: I can't remember what it tasted like.

Richard: It looks like you're doing okay.

Marie: I'm making a mess.

Richard: Maybe the beach isn't the best place.

Marie: I didn't have anywhere else to go.

Richard: I watched you for a while. I didn't realize it was you at first. You looked so . . . exotic sitting out here peeling all of this fruit.

Marie: The skins. There's so many skins. I just keep peeling. And peeling.

Richard: I noticed. *Beat.* I wanted to take a picture, but I left my camera . . . And then I realized I was being ridiculous— you're my wife. So I decided to come over here.

Marie: What if I peel until there's nothing left? Until they're all gone, all of them? What then?

Richard: They won't just disappear. They'll still be here.

Marie: I can't remember what it tasted like.

Richard: Marie. I'm still here. *She looks at him for the first time.*

Marie: Why?

Richard: I didn't know where else to go.

Marie: Keep talking to me.

She lays her head on his lap, still clutching the grapefruit.

Richard: What do you want me to say?

Marie: Something real.

Richard: Real? Well. I'm running my fingers through your hair. I'm not really sure why . . . Susan used to do this for me. It seems like the thing to do right now . . . with your head on my lap. I'm doing it to show affection because you're my wife . . . You're my wife and I'm looking at you and . . . and I can barely see your face . . . For some reason everything is blurry. . . .

Marie sits up and looks at Richard. He continues to stroke her hair.

Marie: I can't remember what you taste like . . .

Richard: . . . But I'm still doing it and I'll keep doing it. They look at each other for a moment and then look out to the ocean. Take a deep breath, Marie.

They both stare out at the ocean, wide awake.

END

Biographies

Sheldon Elter *Métis Mutt*
Sheldon is a Métis actor, writer, and director originally from Northern Alberta. As a stand-up comic, he has emceed and been a host at both Breaker's, and Dave's Comedy Saloon, and toured western Canada twice as the opening comedy act for Hypnotist Marc Savard. His theatre credits include *Undiscover'd Country* (The Undiscover'd Country Collective), *A Prairie Boy's Winter* (Citadel Theatre), *Wrecked* (Azimuth Theatre), *Romeo and Juliet*, *Love's Labour's Lost*, *Twelfth Night* and *Merchant of Venice* (Free Will Players), *Are We There Yet?* and *Carnival Magic/Promise to the Sun* (Concrete Theatre), *Frostbite Christmas* (Stuck in a Snowbank Theatre, Yellowknife), *Wynters' Tale Project*, (To the Moon and Back Productions), *West of the Third Meridian* (Bad Dream Theatre), *Pitchin' A Tent*, (Garrulous Productions), *Othello* (Sound and Fury), and *Red Lips* and *Saturday Night* (Leave it to Jane Theatre). Sheldon is also a core member of Azimuth Theatre's in-house sketch comedy troupe, *Blacklisted*.

Leah Simone Bowen *Code Word: Time*
Leah Simone Bowen is an actor, director and playwright. *Code Word: Time* is the second in a trilogy that includes *The Day Jim Henson Died* and *Playing Small*. Her other plays are: *Pepto Bismol, Rolaids and other sources of light* and *We walk Alone*. Leah has performed with the Second City National Touring Company and was nominated for a 2005 Dora Award in Outstanding Direction for her work on *Thy Neighbour's Wife*. She is co-founder of The IceBox Theatre Company. Leah grew up in Spruce Grove, Alberta and currently lives in Toronto.

Rob Bartel *Beneath the Deep Blue Sky*
Born in Saskatoon, Rob Bartel was the first graduate of the 25th Street Theatre Student Playwright Mentorship Program. Since that time, his award-winning plays have received international acclaim and his poetry has appeared in a variety of Canadian literary magazines. Since 1998, he has been working for BioWare Corp. as a writer

and designer of over a dozen critically acclaimed, best-selling computer and video games. Rob is also a founding member of New Bard Press, publishers of innovative new theatre by emerging artists. He lives with his wife and two pugs on the outskirts of Edmonton.

Kevin Jesuino *Grumplestock's*
A graduate of Grant MacEwan College Theatre Arts Program in 2004, Kevin has experienced most angles of theatre; actor, director, technician and writer. Involved in such productions as *Red Noses*, *A Midsummer's Night Dream*, *The Vampyre* and *The Boys Next Door* and writing for English and Portuguese audiences in Canada, Kevin was featured as a Provincial up-and-coming Theatre Artist at the 2001 Canada Summer Games National Artists Program. Trained in movement, Kevin has attempted to create new works through the art of word and the art of movement. Kevin has also taken part in the Next Generation Arts Festival since 2003 as an actor, dancer, and writer.

Trish Lorenz *Grumplestock's*
Trish graduated from the Grant MacEwan Theatre Arts program in 2004. Before that, she played a lot of basketball, and worked as a personal trainer, basketball coach, and professor. Her first writing project was a solo piece entitled *Ouch!* which was performed at NextFest 2003. Since then, Trish has co-written and performed in *5 Lives of Elizabeth* (Orchard Theatre at the Edmonton Fringe), *Jingle Bell This!* and *Jingle Bell That!* (Bring a Torch Productions), *Reunion of the Century* (Outcast Theatre), and *Suite Murder* (Second Chance Theatre). Trish has also performed with ELOPE and Central Alberta Theatre. Recent highlights include the CKUA radio drama *Guy Faulkrand: Gentleman Adventurer* (Agent Emmerson in *Project Achilles*) and being the public address announcer for the Edmonton Big River Prospects baseball team at Telus Field.

Jon Stewart *Grumplestock's*
Jon Stewart is a playwright/performer from Edmonton. Writing credits include *Little Room* with the Citadel theatre, *Tunnel to China* and *This is Sanctuary* with Nextfest, and *What We Want* with Studio 58. Acting credits include *The Goat, or Who is Sylvia*, *A Christmas Carol* (Citadel Theatre), *Little Room*, *The Dumb Waiter*, *The Love Course* (Edmonton Fringe), and *Blood Brothers* (Walterdale Playhouse). Jon

is a two-time Edmonton Sterling Award nominee, and is currently a student at Studio 58 in Vancouver.

Janis Craft *Citrus*
Janis is a playwright and teaching artist who resides in Chicago, Illinois. She is a fellow of the Edward Albee Foundation and a BFA Playwriting graduate of the Theatre School at DePaul University. Her plays include *Citrus* (New Theater Collective and Theatre Network's Nextfest); *The Smell of Rain When It's Raining*, commissioned by the Children's Theater of Western Springs and developed in collaboration with their High School Repertory company; *Random Acts of Violence In America* (Theatre Network's Nextfest), *Making up the Rules* (Victory Gardens Readers' Theater Series), *Paper Dolls* (Chicago Dramatists Saturday Series), *Between Stops* (Process Theatre at The Urban Institute of Contemporary Arts), *In Search of an Orgasm: The American Way* (The Theatre School Wrights of Spring). Janis has also worked in Chicago and Michigan as a director, dramaturg, choreographer, and producer and has been published as a poet and journalist. In her spare time, Janis curates multimedia art exhibits, studies flamenco, manages a used bookstore, and maintains her literary Internet blogs.

Steve Pirot *Festival Director*
His primary training is as an actor but he also works as a director, playwright, dramaturg, and administrator. He has been nominated for three Elizabeth Sterling Haynes Awards as an actor (*Popcorn*, Citadel Theatre; *Playing Bare*, Theatre Network; *Faithless*, Azimuth Theatre) and once as a playwright (*Faithless* co-written with Chris Craddock). He has a BFA (Acting) and a BA (Drama) from the University of Alberta and also trained with PRIMUS Theatre in Winnipeg. He was born and raised in Edmonton where he lives with his plants. He became Co-Artistic Producer of Azimuth Theatre in 2004. He has been Festival Director for Nextfest: Syncrude Next Generation Arts Festival since 2001 and prior to that he was involved in the Festival as a playwright, actor, dramaturg, talent scout, and booster.

Bradley Moss *Festival Producer and Founder*
Bradley is an award-winning director and actor who has worked across Canada. He is Artistic Director of Theatre Network and the

Producer and Founder of Nextfest: Syncrude Next Generation Arts Festival. Born in Montreal and raised in the Eastern Townships of Quebec, he attended Bishops University where he graduated with an Honours BA in Drama. There he helped initiate and create ACTIV a student drama festival focused on creating new work. After graduation, he moved to Vancouver where he acted in theatre and film and founded the theatre company Big Tree Productions, for which he directed *Provincetown Playhouse*, *Texas Boy* and *Waiting for Godot*. He came to Edmonton in 1992 to begin his MFA in Directing at the University of Alberta, culminating with his thesis play, *The Queens*, produced for Studio Theatre in 1994. The following year, he directed *Stretch* with Andy Curtis and Neil Grahn for the High Performance Rodeo in Calgary and joined Theatre Network to begin work on the development of NextFest as its first festival director and ongoing producer. In the summer of 1996, Bradley directed and independently co-produced *Tony & Tina's Wedding*. In 1998, he performed in Brad Fraser's *Martin Yesterday* for Theatre Network and returned briefly to Montreal to play a leading role in Roy Cross' independent feature film *So Far Away and Blue*. Bradley was appointed Artistic Director of Theatre Network in the spring of 1999. His directing debut for Theatre Network's 1998–99 season was *High Life* by Lee MacDougall, receiving six Elizabeth Sterling Haynes Awards nominations including Outstanding Production and Outstanding Direction. Since then he has directed Wes Borg and Darrin Hagen's *PileDriver!*, George F. Walker's *Problem Child*, Eugene Stickland's *A Guide To Mourning*, Dominic Champagne's *Playing Bare*, Morris Panych's *Lawrence & Holloman*, Michel Tremblay's *For The Pleasure of Seeing Her Again*, Eugene Stickland's *Midlife*, Eugene Stickland's *Excavations*, John Cameron Mitchell's *Hedwig and The Angry Inch*, Martin McDonagh's *A Skull In Connemara*, Eugene Stickland's *All Clear*, Daniel MacIvor's *Marion Bridge*, Michel Tremblay's *Hosanna*, Chris Craddock's adaptation of Miriam Toews' novel *Summer of My Amazing Luck*, Francois Archambault's *The Leisure Society*, Morris Panych's *Girl in The Goldfish Bowl*, and Sam Shepard's *True West*.

Nextfest Anthology highlights five plays from the first five years of The Syncrude Next Generation Arts Festival. This selection is a wacky, quirky, humorous, dark, uplifting, mysterious, and, above all, highly entertaining collection from fresh, young talents.

Nextfest Anthology contains: *SuperEd* by Chris Craddock, *Benedetta Carlini* by Rosemary Rowe, *"No. Please—"* by Sean Callaghan, *The Key to Violet's Apartment* by Paul Matwychuk and *Tuesday and Sundays* by Daniel Arnold with Medina Hahn.

Edited by Glenda Stirling
ISBN 10: 1-896300-37-5
ISBN 13: 978-1-896300-37-5
$18.95 CDN / $12.95 US